Then Nepal's Door Opened

Developing leaders and literature to reach unreached peoples

Alma Hagen

Mega blessings to you!
Joyfully,
Alma Hagen
Revelation 5:9, 7:9-10

xulon PRESS

www.xulonpress.com

Foreword

Alma Hagen has written an important book about one of the most dramatic missionary movements of the twentieth century: the opening of Nepal and the birth and growth of the Nepali church. The number of Nepali believers within Nepal has grown from basically zero in 1950 to well over half a million today. And Alma and her husband Roy have been a significant part of that movement, especially in its beginning.

Most great missionary movements are spearheaded by one or more charismatic evangelists or pastors, whom God uses to open up whole areas to the Gospel. But a critical—though often forgotten—element in the success of any such movement is the discipling of the early national leaders and the provision of basic literature to feed and sustain the newly growing churches. Without training and literature, church movements cannot last, much less thrive.

The Hagens, who arrived in North India even before Nepal's door opened, played a leading role in the training of the first Nepali church leaders and in the preparation of literature for the new churches. Without their work, I doubt the Nepali church would have grown the way it has.

Beyond its missiologic importance, this book also tells the inspiring story of a missionary family and their adventures in the Himalayan Mountains of North India and Nepal. The accounts are vivid and well written. They reveal missionary life as it really is—with all its joys, sorrows, challenges and laughter. Above all, the book tells the story of how God used some ordinary people to accomplish great things to His glory. It was God who opened the door to Nepal and established His church there, and the Hagens were among the chief instruments He used to do it.

Thomas Hale
January 2006

Dedication

I dedicate this book to our five grandchildren,
Timothy, Karis, Kaisa, Nathan, and Anna Joy.
All were born on the mission field,
and all love Jesus.

Prologue

Jesus Christ was born in the Middle East. His life and teachings have reached around the globe. One of his disciples, the Apostle Thomas, traveled to India, where his influence reached far and wide. But his message had not penetrated the Himalayan foothills of Hindu Nepal. Apart from contact with foreign embassies, the door was closed to outside influences. Christians were not welcome in the land.

When the door is slammed in your face, you can turn around and go home—or you can sit on the porch and pray and get ready for when it opens. Darjeeling proved to be our porch on Nepal. Although politically part of India, 80% of the people in the Darjeeling district are ethnically Nepali. They held one key to Nepal.

Followers of Jesus worldwide prayed for Nepal and the spread of the Gospel throughout Asia. Jesus had commanded His followers to go into all the world and to make disciples.

God answered that prayer. *Then Nepal's Door Opened* gives a little glimpse of how God prepared Nepali personnel, Christian literature and literacy materials, to spearhead the furtherance of the Gospel into Nepal. From those mustard seeds, Nepal now has one of the fastest growing churches in the world.

Acknowledgments

Special thanks to the many who encouraged and prayed for me as I wrote this account.

Dr. Lois Esselstrom and Helen Boyd patiently read the manuscript with helpful suggestions.

Our whole Hagen family has been most accommodating, showing daily love and support. Roy has been gracious and patient as I poured over files and letters and wrote and rewrote.

Karl rescued me again and again with his computer expertise. Grandson Timothy, son David, and his wife, the desk-top publisher, Cathy, have been a great asset, spending invaluable hours revising the manuscript.

I thank all those co-workers and prayer partners who have enriched our lives, many of whom show up in the pages of this book.

Most of all, I thank the Lord for His enabling. After all, it's His—story.

> *I will remember the deeds of the Lord.*
> *Yes, I will remember your miracles of long ago.*
> *Psalm 77:13*

Alma Hagen
July 2006

Contents

Table of Contents

Map of Nepal, and Darjeeling, India

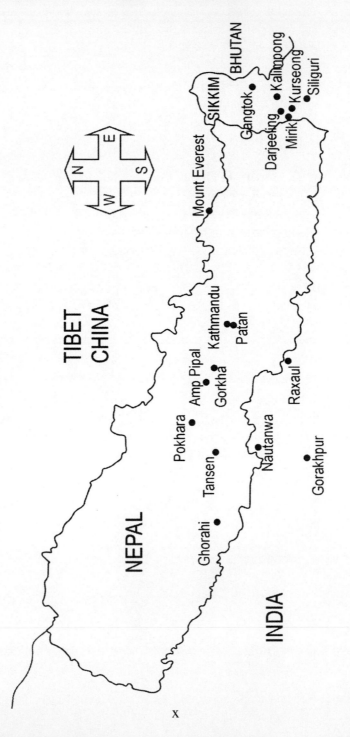

Chapter 1

"Impossible" Commission

The Vow Fulfilled

"Never enter our door again!" Mansubba's brother shouted as he slammed the door in her face. Now she had no place to call home, no place to eat or sleep. She was cast out from her family–all because she had said "I have asked Jesus to come into the open door of my heart. I was baptized last Sunday!" This occurred in Darjeeling, India, in 1952, where freedom of religion was officially guaranteed by the constitution.

But Mansubba was not the only one who experienced a closed door. There was even greater opposition inside Nepal, which declared itself to be a Hindu kingdom. Its laws required that if a person were to change his Hindu religion to another religion, he would be imprisoned in a filthy jail for a year, lose his family inheritance and would again be considered a Hindu. Any person who baptized a new believer or "caused" someone to change his religion would be thrown into prison for six years. Any foreigner considered to be "proselytizing" would be evicted.

Thirty-eight years earlier, in 1914, Ganga Prasad Pradhan and his extended family of more than forty persons had tried to emigrate from Darjeeling, India, back to Kathmandu, where he had been born. They wanted to establish a Christian presence in Nepal. In 1769 AD, Prithwi Narayan Shah had unified Nepal and evicted all foreigners including missionaries. When the authorities discovered Ganga Prasad and his family, they ordered: "Get out! There is no room for Christians in Hindu Nepal." Ganga's whole family was evicted, and they were forced to return to Darjeeling to pray. Nepal's door was again slammed shut to the Gospel.

1

Only three years after Mansubba's radical change, a Nepal Border Fellowship Conference was held in Darjeeling. The keynote speaker, Mr. Oliver, challenged the Nepalis to go to their own homeland. "The need is great. Go into the vineyards . . . the harvest is ripe **now**!"

Four stood up to say "I'll go!" There was 65-year-old Auntie Ruth, frail Manu (short for Mansubba), blind Birendra and slender Pastor D.H. Mukhia. Manu later moved into Nepal to become a very tiny mustard seed planted within the bastion of Hinduism. There would soon be dramatic change in Nepal. But that is only part of the story.

An Unusual Vow

"I'm finished with you!" my own dad snarled as he stood in our partly open door, aiming a double-barreled shotgun down at my mother and me. Our Montana mountain community knew this man as a respected family doctor, but we knew him as the man who struck terror in our hearts. My dad had forced my mother and me to kneel before him on a rough brown mat outside our front door. Momsey remembered the unusual vow she had made long ago. Would it be fulfilled or would we be killed?

We prayed desperately, but silently, knowing that if my dad heard our prayers, he would get angrier. We continued to pray; my dad slowly lowered his gun and stalked away from the door.

My petite mother, Momsey, known to the rest of the world as Frieda Louise Martini, was born on Epiphany Sunday, January 6, 1881. Her godly father, Friederich Wilhelm Martini, was a pastor to newly arrived immigrants on Ellis Island in New York City. He and his wife had two other children. My uncle Carl became an engineer for the city of Chicago. My aunt Elizabeth Alma, nicknamed Else, became one of the first women architects in America.

The Martini ancestors had emigrated from Holland to Germany in 1746 and from Germany to America in the late 1800's. Their daily use of German proved a valuable asset to Frieda.

As a child, Frieda loved to play the piano and write poetry. Completing high school, she trained as a nurse in hopes of going overseas for mission work. She applied for volunteer service in India, only to be rejected because the doctor felt she was not strong enough for such an arduous task. Frieda was devastated. Then she made a vow, a daring act of faith. "Lord, if I ever marry and have children, I give them to you now for your service." Would she ever fulfill that vow?

On finishing her Masters degree at Oberlin University, she taught at Northwestern University in Evanston, Illinois. Then Germany declared war on Russia. In 1916 an American physician's expedition prepared to go to Graudens, Germany. It was financed by the American German Relief Society to care for wounded soldiers. Frieda was chosen to be the unit's secretary, interpreter and news reporter. She sent firsthand accounts of the unit's happenings to a German newspaper published in New York.

Than came the grim news that Germany and the United States had

broken off relations. Frieda's unit returned to Chicago before being trapped in the war. There she found a letter from a German-born Dr. Buchen, printed with a baronial crest. The doctor had learned that his brother, a Lt. Commander fighting on the Russian front, had been injured and might possibly be taken to the Fortress Hospital in Graudens. He enclosed a photo, asking if she recalled seeing a patient, his brother, who strongly resembled him.

Frieda wrote, "I regret that I cannot recall a patient resembling you, but shall send your photo and letter to our chief surgeon in Massa-

Alma's mother, Frieda Martini Buchen, made a sacrificial vow that God fulfilled through Alma.

3

chusetts. I trust he remembers your brother and can give the desired information."

The following week another letter arrived from the doctor, stating that he had just learned that his brother died en route to Graudens. Thus began a correspondence between Frieda and the doctor, "Freiherr Baron von Buchen." He described his practice among the western mountain folk, his delights at the beauty of Montana's mountains, so similar to his home in Buchen, Westphalia, in the Rhineland of western Germany, and his hunting and fishing there. He loved music and singing. Frieda enjoyed playing the piano and understood the medical challenges he faced.

Dr. Buchen, Alma's father

Then one day a letter came proposing that Frieda come to Montana to marry him. Because she had never met him, nor had any assurance that he was a Christian, her devout family was deeply concerned. They pleaded with her not to be "unequally yoked," as God's Word warns, nor to be hasty in her decisions.

Frieda's concerned father wrote to a pastor in Montana, asking about the doctor. He replied, "Dr. Buchen has a frank, friendly way about him, and most of his patients are devoted to him. Some almost swear by him. But I strongly doubt whether he would be a fit life-partner for a Christian lady. Not a professing Christian, he is occasionally profane and sometimes drinks."

"Then this is someone I must lead to Christ!" came Frieda's

argument. So against her family's advice and scriptural direction, Frieda went off to Montana to marry Dr. Buchen, a man eighteen years older than she.

It wasn't long before she discovered he could show two very different personalities. When he was in a good mood, he was jolly, fun-loving and entertaining. When he was angry or drunk, he could be hateful and violent.

Frieda prayed continually for him. She soon realized her folly of thinking that she could bring him to Christ. Only the Holy Spirit could do that. One of her own poems best describes her new life:

GLORY WITHIN

Tears set to music,
That was all my song,
When first grief's cloud o'er shadowed me.
Then, through the door of pain,
I saw a heart of love:
A thorn-crowned brow,
A nail-pierced hand.
The cross burst into meaning!
>   Cloud, you have cleared my vision,
>   And now I bless you!

Frieda Martini Buchen

Her husband intentionally caused her to miscarry three pregnancies. During her fourth pregnancy, Frieda, now forty-three, managed to slip away by train to her sister Else in Michigan to await the arrival of her child.

"It's a little lady," said the doctor as the baby was delivered. I was that baby. When I was three weeks old, Momsey boarded the train to take me back to Montana and to my dad.

I grew up having a love-hate relationship with my father. If he was in a good mood, I relaxed. If he was in an angry mood, I slipped out of his sight as quickly as I could.

Momsey and I prayed fervently, daily, for my father's conversion. I had gone forward at age four to give my heart to Jesus in response to a chalk-talk presentation at the nearby Baptist church. I had been able to join her in prayer and faith since then.

Then Nepal's Door Opened

Life in Darby was simple. Back of the house was a woodshed where we chopped wood on a big round sawed-off tree trunk. It was my job to keep the kitchen woodbox full so Momsey could cook on the iron stove. Patients coming to see my Dad took a boardwalk that led around the house to his office, which was fully equipped with operating table and glassed-in cases of instruments. We stored ice in sawdust in the barn. One chunk, carried in large wide tongs, kept our little icebox cold for several days.

Our Christmas tree was decorated with gilded walnuts, cookies, and delicate German ornaments. Clip-on holders held five-inch candles. Miraculously we had no fires from lit candles.

Dad, a genuine German, made his own beer with malt and hops in a huge crock. He made me siphon the warm beer into bottles and place them in the narrow space between the kitchen stove and the wall to ferment. Only fear of his reprisals kept me from spitting out that horrible-tasting brew.

On a beautiful spring day when I was ten, Momsey and I were out in our apple orchard praying. When we came into the house through my Dad's office, we found him kneeling before his big leather chair. He was pouring out his heart to the Lord, confessing his sins and asking for forgiveness. What a day of rejoicing that was! The whole atmosphere of our home was transformed. My father stopped drinking, smoking and swearing. Gone was his terrible temper. He was truly a changed person. He had come to repentance and faith through reading Dwight L. Moody's book, *Peace with God*, and E. Stanley Jones's book, *The Christ of the Indian Road*.

Two years later Dad died of a heart attack.

In order to support the two of us, Momsey went back to teaching. She taught English and German at Billings Polytechnic Institute. There we lived in faculty accommodations on the campus. I soon had many friends in high school as well as in the Institute. It wasn't long before I was dancing *Roll out the barrel, we'll have a barrel of fun* along with the college students. At the same time I was very active in Luther League, declaring my intentions of being a missionary!

But Momsey was very concerned. She wanted me to have a safer Christian environment. Just before my senior year, a door opened for her to teach English and German at a Christian school, Augustana

Academy, in Canton, South Dakota. My pastor was strongly opposed to my attending the Academy and offered to keep me in the parsonage with his family if only I would stay in Billings. I decided to move with Momsey to Canton.

It was the custom for the school to have a "Prayer and Praise Week" to which special speakers were invited. One morning in chapel during that week I was singing the hymn, *Thy life was given for me, what have I given Thee?* The words I sang pierced my heart. I had given my heart to Jesus but I was "in the driver's seat," doing just what I wanted to do. Quietly, but very determinedly, I surrendered my whole life to the Lord, to will what He willed, to go where He wanted me to go.

After chapel I ran upstairs to tell my Momsey of my decision to follow the Lord whole-heartedly wherever He wanted me to go. With tears in her eyes, she told me of her vow to give whatever children God would give her back to Him for His service. The Lord had heard and was answering her prayer. She composed for me:

YOUR MOTHER'S FAITH

Over somber mountain ranges,
　　Wreathed in veils of mist,
Falls the night, while Goldhead's calm
　　Dreaming, slumber-kissed.
Mother love alone is waking,
　　Mother's praying hands
With their quiet strength envelope
　　Future's distant lands.

Alma, with your floral beauty,
　　Child of fervent prayers,
When the dazzling world assails you
　　With alluring airs,
Will you then be true to Jesus
　　Till your latest breath,
Brave to suffer, strong to conquer,
　　True, dear heart, till death?
Wheresoever you are guided
　　By your heavenly Friend,

7

Mother's prayers will ever follow
Onward to the end!

Frieda Martini Buchen

Open Door to Love

One of Momsey's associate teachers at the Academy was Bernice Gullickson, affectionately known as Bunny by her English students. She felt called as a missionary to the Afghan people.

After I graduated from the Academy, she invited me to accompany her to the Lutheran Deeper Life Conference at Medicine Lake, Minnesota, just outside Minneapolis. We were standing at the rough-hewn registration desk when the door opened opposite us. In walked handsome, blue-eyed, blond Roy Hagen. My heart did a double flip. During the week-long conference and while waiting in line for meals, there were occasional chances to chat. I found him shy and retiring, but a very committed Christian. The conference focused on knowing and walking with Jesus in a deeper measure.

After the conference Bunny said, "Let's go visit a Jewish children's camp outside of St. Paul. A dear old Mrs. Walgren is running the camp there." Who should be working at that camp but Roy Hagen! Just before Bunny and I left, he handed me a small booklet entitled *Himself* by A.B. Simpson. When I had a quiet moment, I took it out to read. It showed me that **everything** I needed was all wrapped up in Jesus Himself. That tract spoke clearly to my heart as I proceeded back home.

I sent off a little thank-you note for the booklet. A speedy reply from Roy said, "I don't recall what you look like. Please send me a photo." So much for first impressions! I sent off a photo and thus began a life-changing correspondence.

Roy was of Norwegian descent. His father, Christian Anderson Hagen, was born in 1889 in Norway's western Trondheim. During difficult Norwegian winters the family's diet was reduced to potatoes and milk. He skied seven miles to school. His father died when Christian was only thirteen. The next year, lemmings, small arctic rodents, invaded the Trondheim area. Some lemmings fell into the well at Christian's home while others rushed down into the ocean. Not realizing that the water was contaminated, his mother drank the well water and died soon after.

A kindly pastor took orphaned Christian into his family. He learned tailoring until he was nineteen. He saved the equivalent of twenty-five American dollars, the amount required to emigrate to America, and proceeded to Minneapolis knowing little English.

Roy's mother, Ingeborg, was from Osterdalen, Norway. A coal mine opened in Osterdalen drawing many rough characters. Ingeborg's parents were concerned for their beautiful, auburn-haired, sixteen-year-old daughter. They chose to send her to relatives living in Hudson, Wisconsin. Christian and Ingeborg met at a baptism of friends. Not long afterward they were married in Minneapolis in 1910.

Then came the difficult Depression. Chris and Ingeborg strove to keep their tailoring business afloat, but earnings were skimpy. Learning that the government offered free land for development, Chris and Ingeborg became settlers one hundred miles north of Minneapolis near Cloverton. On weekends Chris drove his three pedaled Model T Ford from Minneapolis to Cloverton. He would dynamite and fell trees, clear land, build a house and plant a garden, and then return to tailoring on Mondays. Roy was born in Cloverton, the youngest of four sons. His brothers pulled him to school on a sled when he was only four.

But soon the family moved back to Minneapolis where a daughter, Evelyn, was born. Growing up, Roy was active in Concordia Lutheran Church, renamed Holy Triune Lutheran Church. He was so hungry for God that he attended a midweek Bible Study in a neighboring church. Through studying Galatians 3:13-14, he was convicted of sin, repented, and came to assurance of salvation. That gave a fresh focus to his spiritual life.

A boys' team, the Knights of Luther, was organized at Concordia. Roy, Harold Brokke, and two brothers, Ken and Bud Roufs, part of that team, formed a bond that lasted many years. The team visited churches, singing and witnessing. Roy became the first one of the congregation to go into full-time Christian ministry. Harold Brokke went on to have an important role at Bethany Fellowship.

For several summers Roy helped relatives in North Dakota. An intense drought there was so severe that for seven years no farm machinery was taken out. Wearing inner tubes to his thighs, he would stand on a load of freshly cut, green Russian thistles and spread them out, fodder for horses.

Other summers the Roufs brothers and Roy worked on a truck

farm, picking beans for seventy-five cents a day, sometimes in 107°F (42°C) temperatures. He was determined to do his job, even when others quit. That determination served him in good stead in years to come.

Slight of build, Roy was often at the top of gymnastic pyramids in high school, as well as the top of his class scholastically in high school and college. But there was one thing that captivated Roy's heart and interests more than thistles, pyramids and good grades. That was Christ's compelling command to go into all the world, preach the Gospel, and make disciples of all nations.

In the early 1940's, Roy was part of Lutheran World Crusade, a like-minded group that had its roots in the awakening led by Hans Nielsen Hauge in Norway. These believers were also challenged by the Moravian Mission movement, started by Count Zinzendorf. The Moravians had maintained a round-the-clock prayer vigil for a hundred years.

Those in Lutheran World Crusade gathered to learn about and share a common vision and burden for the "closed" lands of Central Asia: Tibet, Nepal, Bhutan, Baluchistan and Afghanistan. In these lands the good news of salvation through Jesus had not yet been made known.

Lutheran World Crusade joined the World Mission Prayer League (WMPL). Persistent, determined, faith-filled prayer based on God's promises was the foundation for the group of mission-minded people. It became a channel through which lay people could reach beyond established mission fields and budgets to reach unreached areas. My teacher, Bunny, was a member of the World Mission Prayer League and introduced me to the Mission leaders.

After I graduated from Augustana Academy, Momsey and I moved to Ft. Wayne, Indiana where I enrolled at Indiana University Extension. The next summer I returned to Minneapolis, hungry to know God better. I spent an afternoon with Pastor Dahle who helped me repent of pride and a whole list of sins that grieved the Lord. He showed me from Romans 6 that I could daily reckon myself dead to sin and alive unto Jesus. My joy and release knew no bounds.

Still rejoicing, I boarded the train for Chicago where I had a summer job with the Lutheran Children's Home Finding Society. Four of us worked mostly with children from broken homes. In the evenings we sang at city mission meetings, studied God's Word, and prayed much for the children.

August 19, 1944, became a red-letter day. That night at 2 a.m., my co-worker, Margaret Birkedal, came to the place where she prayed, "Lord, I surrender my will, my life, my all, to you to be yours one hundred percent." She became a changed person. Thus began a beautiful friendship that has lasted decades across half the world down through three generations. Little did we dream that we would one day be working together overseas.

I wrote a round-robin letter to my classmates of Augustana Academy quoting a poem by Amy Carmichael of Dohnavur, India, that showed the longing of my heart:

> Jesus, Redeemer and my One Inspirer,
>   Heat in my coldness, set my life aglow,
> Break down my barriers, draw, yea, draw me nigher,
>   Thee would I know, whom it is life to know.
>
> Deepen me, rid me of the superficial,
>   From pale delusion set my spirit free;
> All my interior being quick unravel,
>   Pluck forth each thread of insincerity.
> Thy vows are on me, O to serve Thee truly,
>   Love perfectly, in purity obey—
> Burn, burn, O Fire; O Wind, now winnow thoroughly
>   O Sword, awake against the flesh and slay.
>
> O that in me
>   Thou, my Lord, may see
> Of the travail of Thy soul,
>   And be satisfied.
>
> *Amy Carmichael*

Margaret returned to St. Olaf College, where one day she noticed someone reading his Bible in the library. She stopped to inquire of a Bible Study on campus. That devout student was Harold Brokke, a close friend of Roy's. He invited Margaret to visit Ted Hegre's home meeting in Minneapolis. This meeting was the beginning of the far-reaching Bethany Fellowship International, where Harold later taught and eventually became president.

Then Nepal's Door Opened

Meanwhile, for three and a half years Roy and I corresponded and saw each other for a week or two in the summer. After two years at Ft. Wayne, I transferred to Carthage College for my last two years. In 1946, Roy and I both went to the first big missions conference organized by InterVarsity Christian Fellowship, held in Toronto, Ontario, between Christmas and the New Year. Roy had come from Minneapolis and I had come from Ft. Wayne. During that week, a historic ice storm created a winter wonderland bathed in tinkling, glassy ice. In his pocket Roy brought a beautiful ring. We were engaged at that conference, which later became the famous biannual Urbana Missions gatherings.

The next summer we were married, August 16, 1947. Harold Brokke was in our wedding party. Margaret Birkedal sang *Our Goal is God Himself.*

Our first Christmas card after we were married pictured us pointing to West China. The World Mission Prayer League (WMPL) had a team of six working in Western China among the Tibetans. We were hoping we could go to Central Asia. Would that card ever come to fulfillment?

Roy was assigned by Luther Seminary to an internship at the very traditional St. Olaf Lutheran Church in Detroit. I worked in the Lutheran Charities, doing secretarial work mornings and visiting hospital patients in the afternoon. Ruth Hauge (Fullilove) had just returned from Darjeeling, India, where she studied Urdu, preparing to go to Pakistan. She came to visit us and to speak on missions at St. Olaf.

As she spoke of the Nepali church in Darjeeling, I was sure that was where we were to go. But I didn't say a word to Roy. "If this is of God, He will show Roy," I thought. A few months later Roy came to breakfast saying, "I dreamed we were packing up to go to Nepal!" God was confirming His direction for us. We would go to work among the Nepalis. The door was opening for fulfillment of Momsey's prayer, so well expressed in her poem:

> Launch upon the sea of faith,
>   May no angry billows frighten!
> Let His love imbue your heart,
>   His "Well done!" your voyage brighten,
> And in brotherly accord

Keep your eyes upon the Lord!
Launch upon the thorny path
Leading on to lofty vision,
Like the holy men of old,
Who with dauntless, firm decision,
Brandishing the Spirit's sword,
Bravely followed Christ, the Lord!
Launch upon the Master's work,
Giving Him the honor, glory;
Hold aloft His blazing torch,
Telling forth salvation's story.
Christian, count no cost too high
For your Lord to testify!

Frieda Martini Buchen

Called to Wait?

Although we were called to the Nepali people, mountains loomed in our way. The first big obstacle was pressure to go to an already established mission field.

The goal of WMPL was to take the Gospel to unreached people groups. That goal was not well understood among those involved with long-established mission churches. They tended to perpetuate themselves rather than hand over the work to local pastors and move onto new groups. This policy straight-jacketed mission leaders, preventing them from penetrating unreached areas.

When Roy's missions professor learned we wanted to reach Nepal, he quizzed Roy, "What's the use of sitting outside of the closed door of a Hindu kingdom? They forbid conversions. Only two out of a hundred people can read. Why not go to Madagascar? At least there is an established work there."

"God has called us to those who have never heard the Good News of Jesus. I must be obedient," Roy replied. The professor shrugged and walked off. He never dreamed what God would do in Nepal in the next fifty years.

Both Roy and I knew Jesus had called us to go to the Nepalis and make disciples. His call would hold us steady through the thick and thin of learning the language and living in a different culture. We were being sent by Jesus and He would see us through sickness and even apparent failure as we worked with a variety of personalities from many different national backgrounds. Ours was a calling to be humble servants, to live by prayer, faith, love and giving as we joyfully, obediently partnered with Him. But first we had more challenges to overcome.

Roy and several others traveled to Wisconsin to share the mission vision. I was staying with Roy's folks when I suddenly realized that our expected baby was arriving shortly. When I phoned the doctor, he said, "You get straight to Deaconess Hospital right away!" I jumped into the car and "Grandpa Chris" drove speedily toward the hospital. "Ya, I've heard about too many of dese babies born in taxi cabs!" he declared in his gentle Norwegian brogue—as he whizzed right past the hospital. It didn't take him long to turn around, and very shortly David was born—**in** the hospital.

Nepal lies sandwiched between two giants, India and Tibet (now claimed by China). Thousands of Nepalis had spilled over from Nepal into India's Darjeeling District on the eastern border of Nepal, many to work in Darjeeling's tea gardens.

To "sit outside the closed door," for us, meant to go to Darjeeling to learn the Nepali language and culture. We were accepted by the World Mission Prayer League as part of a team of seven missionaries applying for visas to India.

While we waited for the visas, Roy finished seminary, took a Wycliffe Bible Translators' linguistics course, and was ordained as interim pastor to two small congregations in Iowa. We collected big blue fifty-five-gallon steel drums and began packing plastic dishes, clothes for five years, and books for translation work. We carefully painted "our" Darjeeling address on the barrels by faith and shipped them off to the coast. And we prayed!

Our second obstacle came after we were all packed up. Warm-hearted Iowa farm folk gave us a royal send-off for Darjeeling as we started for the East Coast. What a surprise awaited us as we stopped in Chicago. "SIX VISAS REFUSED, JEANETTE STOELTING'S APPLICATION APPROVED." We were stunned at this telegram! We were learning that when Jesus says, "Go into all the world," he sometimes says, "Wait!" It was clear we were to wait.

We continued to pray for the Lord of the harvest to open the door to which He had called us. We had to declare by faith that Jesus was greater than any closed doors. It was a time of waiting and depending on God. My Momsey stood with us, cheering us on.

We felt we should continue on to the East Coast. A good friend took us under his wing in his parsonage and gave us his Ford car. There was one difficulty with that car—we had to add a quart of oil every thirteen miles. But we had wheels! In a few weeks we proceeded to the Kennedy School of Missions in Hartford, Connecticut. There Roy enrolled to study Indian History and Culture and India's classical literary language, Sanskrit.

For his Master's thesis, Roy wrote the history of the World Mission Prayer League. I struggled with carbon paper to type four clean letter perfect copies. We were wonderfully encouraged by learning of the myriad ways in which God had previously provided for WMPL workers on three continents: central Africa, central Asia, and the heart of South America. All these people were living by faith and obedience to the Lord.

We were living out that reality of God's provision even as Roy wrote about it. WMPL's financial policy was for each missionary to trust God to supply his living expenses. Unsolicited gifts and contributions were sent to the mission office and then forwarded to the overseas field. This made up our basic allowance, which was enough for a simple lifestyle. But this allowance began only after we arrived on the field. Until then, we were totally dependent on the Lord for everything as we waited, studied, and lived in Hartford. Occasionally Roy was asked to conduct a church service. Gifts came from family or friends that helped pay for tuition, food and gas. What answers to prayer!

One Sunday at church we were introduced to a factory worker called Pearl. She invited us to stay in her guest bedroom and share her kitchen. After we arrived at her home she pointed to the patch of big spinach-like leaves. "See that big garden of Swiss chard. Help yourself. Eat all you want!" What a provision! We dined on Swiss chard soup, Swiss chard salad, and Swiss chard hot dish. Like Elijah who was fed by God at the Kerith brook, we experienced God's provision of a simple menu.

Later we moved to a location much closer to the Kennedy School of Missions. This time we shared a home with a very congenial couple, Paul and Jane. Jane was a stone-deaf nurse with a large, warm heart. Whenever she saw a cloud of blue from the oil-burning Ford coming down the road she stuttered, "Oh, the 'Mininister' is coming," and pretended to dust the furniture.

Our second son Paul was born while we lived in Hartford. The year passed quickly. We applied to India again for visas and waited. Roy completed his masters degree. We headed back to Minneapolis, our mission base.

En route we stopped off to see Momsey, now a frail little widow of seventy. She was still teaching German and French at Marion College in Marion, Indiana. She was delighted to have us and her grandchildren stay overnight. In the morning, I asked my usual, "Did you sleep well, Momsey?"

"No" she said. "I had a terrible battle! But God said to me, 'If I had only one Son and could give Him up for the world, can't you give your only child up for Me?'" Then with a twinkle in her hazel eyes, she said, "When I said 'Yes!' then I could sleep."

It wasn't easy to leave Momsey alone. She had no other family to care for her. She was willing to let me go. That gave me courage to also trust God for her. I knew that as I obeyed the Lord, He promised to provide for all her needs. Several of the poems Momsey wrote best describe her stalwart faith:

DIVINE GIRDING

Leaning on Messiah's arm,
   Folded in His healing peace,
Frail, but nurtured, energized,
   By His mighty love's release,—
Heaven's eternal powers surge
   Through a heart thus yielded, still,
He will keep it evermore,
   In the current of His will. [1]

Frieda Martini Buchen

COURAGE !

Beyond things tossed and shaken
   The Everlasting stands,
To bring to pass His marvels,
   With strong, unerring hands!
Behold, He goes before us,
   On stony pilgrim path,

Reviving our allegiance,
    Restoring valiant faith.

For nothing can dismay us,
    If God ordains it so,
And lives poured out for Jesus
    His reinforcement know.
Then, warriors for the highest,
    Go on from strength to strength!
Jehovah is your captain,
    And He will win at length.[1]

Frieda Martini Buchen

There was not a trace of a "pity party" in her sending us off. Rather, like Hannah of old, she gave us away in joyful assurance of the fulfillment of that vow of long ago.

We drove on to Minneapolis to Roy's family and WMPL headquarters. There a yellow telegram brought word that all six visas to India had at last been granted. The door to India had opened! We were off to the unaccustomed and unfamiliar.

Into the Unfamiliar

We hoisted anchor at Seattle on a Dutch freighter for a six-week voyage across the Pacific. There were fourteen passengers. We docked at Vancouver to load on more freight and then we were off. A few days later a terrible storm rocked the *S.S. Slamat* from side to side like a cork on a big wave. I was miserably sea sick. Seven-month-old Paul was in a baby basket on the floor next to my bunk where I had collapsed.

A waiter set a tray of tea, Dutch rusks and apple sauce on the table next to the basket. When the ship suddenly pitched to one side, the tea, rusks and applesauce all landed on Paul. I looked at my applesauce-covered baby and just groaned. Fortunately he had no serious aftereffects.

After three weeks of salt spray and seeing only water, we were

---

[1] Lutheran Herald. Used by permission.

happy to see the Philippine Islands on the horizon. While we docked in Cebu to unload freight, a kindly lady from Texas took us on a tour of the city. She offered us French vanilla ice cream. What a treat after raw bacon for breakfast! Mission manuals had warned, "Avoid ice cream and ice cubes!" However, she had lived in Cebu for twenty years. We felt she should know what was safe to eat. Alas, a few days out of Cebu, I came down with a 104°F temperature and bacillary dysentery, a true introduction to Asia. I learned the hard way that mission manuals meant what they said.

One afternoon I felt I must write some letters to be posted at the next port of call.

"Honey, please watch David while I take Paul to the cabin and write some letters."

"Sure, I'll be glad to," he replied.

An hour later I climbed back up on deck to see how Roy and David were faring.

Roy was intently reading a book—and David was nowhere in sight. The horizontal bars around the deck left a lot of room for a two-

Roy, David, Alma and Paul were welcomed at the gangplank by Millie Hasselquist and Becky Grimsrud.

year-old to slip through and fall overboard.

"Where's David, Roy?" I queried.

He hadn't a clue. We searched frantically. Finally, two decks below us, we found David in the middle of a coil of rope, playing peek-a-boo with the sailors.

Our ship shuddered to a stop as we docked in Calcutta on David's second birthday in November 1951. As we started down the gangplank, we heard a cheery, "Welcome to India!" Millie Hasselquist and Becky Grimsrud had come down to meet us. India! I was finally fulfilling the unusual vow my mother had made long ago.

We climbed into a small taxi to go to a hotel. We were soon introduced to the harshness of life in Calcutta, a city of squalor and wealth, misery and industry. The smell of incense, urine, and diesel exhaust filled the air. Sacred cows fed on discarded vegetables along the side of the road or napped in the street. Clanging streetcars missed jaywalking pedestrians by a hair. Vendors hawked habit-forming betel nut. Street-side barbers squatted, lathering their customers for a shave. Thousands made their only home right on the sidewalk. I learned that such a lifestyle was considered but "*maya*," an illusion, according to Hindu thought.

We had modest accommodations while waiting for our luggage to clear customs. When I asked the waiter to please bring some milk for baby Paul, he gave a quick jerk of his head to the left. I took it as a shrug of "who cares," only to have him turn up a few minutes later with the milk. That quick jerk of his head turned out to be an Indian nod saying, "OK." At lunch a Bengali at the adjoining table loudly slurped his soup. Another belched loudly. "Such bad manners!" I critically thought to myself. Later, I learned that according to Bengali custom slurping and belching indicates you find the food delicious! We had much to learn.

As we walked through the market, we saw a shelf for Hindu deities in many shops. The images had eyes that could not see, ears that could not hear and mouths that could not speak. We ached for the people to know the Living God who could see everything, who could hear their cries for help, and who wanted to reveal His love to them.

Then came our first Indian train trip. I stood in numb disbelief as I saw two porters walking toward the baggage car carrying one of our heavy blue drums horizontally on their heads. Whenever the train stopped at a station, we heard the hot tea vendors crying, *"Garam cha,*

Garam cha." They sold sweet hot tea in small cone-shaped pottery cups. It was safer drinking tea than water.

Finally we reached Siliguri, the railhead near Darjeeling. Our luggage was transferred to a truck and we piled into a land rover to begin our trip up into the Himalayan foothills. We drove through well-groomed tea gardens, gradually leaving the lush green tropical plains and gaining altitude on countless zigzags scratched into the steep hillsides. The area definitely became more temperate, the air cooler, thinner and cleaner.

As we ascended, Millie and Becky pointed out the Nepalis along the road. Beautiful women with jet black hair, long-sleeved blouses covered with a shawl, and floor-length garb squatted in front of their homes right on the side of the road. The men had colorful cloth caps worn at an angle, jackets and baggy cotton trousers, tight from the knee to the ankle, like jodhpurs. The children appeared scantily clad, considering it was the end of November and cold. These were the people to whom our Father had sent us.

After taking three hours to crawl up 48 miles we turned a corner. Suddenly there was Darjeeling, with massive, snow-capped Mt. Kanchenjunga looming above it, dwarfing everything else in view. When we arrived in the city, we had to adjust to the altitude of 6,500 ft. We climbed slowly up another two hundred feet to St. Joseph's Mount, our home for the next two years. I was again amazed as Tibetan porters carried our heavy fifty-five-gallon drums of belongings up the hill on their backs held by a strap slung over their foreheads and down around the barrels.

Millie and Becky returned to their ministry in Mirik, a two-hour, twenty-six mile drive away. We joined Gordon and Millie Bell and Clarence and Helen Hjelmervik. They had recently fled from West China, escaping the advancing Communist Chinese army. Lillian Carlson and Dorothy Christiansen had also come from West China and were now settled in Kalimpong. Each family had two rooms and a bath. We shared a kitchen attached to the outside of the building on the ground floor.

We had a week to get oriented, unpack, learn our way around town and then settle down to language study. Our co-workers arranged for Dan Mit (pronounced "done-meet") to care for David and Paul while we spent eight hours a day learning Nepali. Dan Mit was one of the fair-skinned Lepcha, an ethnic group originally from Sikkim, north of Darjeeling District. She was a tiny young lady who always covered her head with a shawl and had yards and yards of material around her waist above her long skirt. Her bare feet padded softly as she faithfully tended to our children.

Our efforts to learn Nepali and distinguish its four different d's and four different t's (dental and reflexive, unaspirated and aspirated) were humbling and hilarious! The cook barely let on when I mistakenly told him to brown the rat (*musa*) instead of the meat (*masu*) or to slice the dog (*kukur*) instead of the cucumber (*kakra*). We learned to laugh at ourselves. Along with language learning, the three men of the mission took turns teaching Bible studies to Nepali young men with the aim to train Nepalis to minister to their own people.

On Christmas Eve we were invited downstairs to the Bells' for the children's special dinner of soft-cooked eggs, strained squash, toast, and red jello—a real treat in Darjeeling. When all the smudgy hands were wiped off and the crumbs brushed away, we gave out presents to the children. David squealed with delight over his top. Paul promptly popped his rattle into his mouth to sooth teething gums. Long after the children were tucked in, I tiptoed back into their room to hear David

Darjeeling at the foot of Mt Kanchenjunga.
Photo Courtesy of Das Studio.

whisper a sweet "Thank you, Mommy" as though he had been lying there reflecting on the wonders of his red top and the joy of Christmas.

Lillian Carlson and Dorothy Christiansen, working with Tibetans in Kalimpong, had come to Darjeeling for the holiday. Christmas morning Lillian declared, "There was a rat in our room last night. What should I do if he gets into my sleeping bag?" The mission manuals hadn't discussed that emergency. Lillian was relieved to have a rat trap placed in her room the next night.

The following morning, four of us made our way 750 feet down to the TB Sanatorium to visit a Nepali Christian, Shilling Mukhia. He had been raised in a Christian home in the midst of a Hindu environment, but his life floundered in the mire of sin. His father, a pharmacist in the government hospital, was often dismayed at his son's behavior. His mother prayed that his darkness would turn to light. His drinking and carousing had brought shame to his home.

Then one day Shilling and friend Andrew were gloriously converted. Shilling's destiny was changed, but that was only part of unexpected happenings. All within a year, two of his four children and his wife died, and the doctor pronounced him a pulmonary tubercular case in the last stage. There was little hope for him, yet he was joyfully witnessing to his fellow Hindu patients about the wonderful difference Jesus had made in his life. God had begun a deep work. Little did he dream of the important role he would play in the future pioneer work in Nepal.

Between Christmas and New Years we had a field conference of all WMPL workers. There was a beautiful spirit of love and unity as we prayed together and sought God's strategy for the best way to minister Jesus' love to the Nepalis. We listened to a message recorded on wire that Roy and I brought with us by our Director Paul Lindell. Paul spoke on God's providing His new missionary, the Apostle Paul, with a window (a vision), a basket (a means of getting out and working), and a rope (gently held with loving, helpful hands when the whole city was barricaded against him). As a team we reflected about how God had similarly provided for us.

We had a vision for training Nepalis to reach their own people with the Gospel. The Lord had brought us to Darjeeling for that purpose. We had met one unforgettable Nepali and we would soon meet another. There were many praying for us in our homeland. We were encouraged.

Chapter 2

Encountering Asia

Light as Snow

He was no ordinary man, this gentleman from Nepal. To Nepalis he was known as Pooba Manab. To our team he was *Sadhuji*, which means "respected holy man."

He had been upset by the social injustice and political slavery of his people in Nepal. When he spoke out on these issues he landed in a Nepali jail as a political prisoner. His life seemed fruitless. While he was in prison, someone poked a book of prayers of different religions through the bars. "Read it!" the friend begged.

He took the book and began to read. He read, "But when you pray, go into your room and shut the door and pray to your Father who is in secret, and your Father who sees in secret will reward you."[2]

Who was this? Who said this? For whom was it said? Who was this "Father" who wanted fellowship with His children? Who was this Father who listens, answers and rewards? It all sounded so good, so real, so simple, so personal. He had to pursue this. So he put together a prayer. "God, called Father, I have read your instruction and bring my petitions to you. Release me from jail, restore my favor with the authorities, and give me the necessities for living."

Within a short time he was released from prison, a friend met him on the street and offered him lodging and food, and he was restored to favor by the authorities. Later he described his experience as a man throwing a rope out of the window into the dark and someone out there caught the rope and pulled. He knew the "God called Father" had answered his prayer. On leaving prison he managed to find a Bible in Hindi, the language of North India.

Since then he had searched diligently. Seekers came to him begging for religious enlightenment, but he turned them away saying, "How can the blind lead the blind?"

He, his wife and children came to Darjeeling to open a school in

---

[2] Matt.6:6 RSV

23

his home. His friends in Kathmandu, Nepal's capital, were so impressed with his brilliance that they sent their sons all the way to Darjeeling to enroll in his school. He chose to teach only boys, but some girls were so eager to learn that they cut their hair and donned boys' clothes.

Hunched over with a heavy gray blanket covering his shoulders, he unfolded his dramatic life. His name was known far and wide by many who looked to him for spiritual guidance. Fluent in several

languages, he had gone to gurus and weighed and pondered religious writings in some of the most noted religious centers in India. He had tried many forms of prayer and fasting. He tried desperately to improve his moral fervor, his self sacrifice. He could quote Buddhist and Hindu scriptures and explain their meaning. He had joined the quiet of an isolated monastery for some time to quell the desires in his soul, to reach Nirvana and become a "drop of water joining the ocean." But he came only to spiritual bankruptcy. All he found was a muddy moral stream within him.

Now in Darjeeling a foreign woman wanted to improve her already excellent Nepali. He agreed to give Millie Hasselquist advanced language lessons. But more importantly, she knew this Father of whom he had read, this living

Sadhuji felt as light as snow after trusting in Christ.

24

God. Then our WMPL Director, Paul Lindell, came to Darjeeling and spent much time with Sadhuji, opening the meaning of the Bible to him. Paul described an afternoon with Sadhuji:

> *"We were sitting together in a corner near the fireplace. The chill afternoon shadows deepened unnoticed into night and the blazing fire crumbled slowly into warm ashes as we plunged into the Book of God. Page after page, and passage after passage opened before us like doors and windows. We seemed to be sitting upon the very threshold of another world. Not a world off yonder in space, but right at hand, all about us. His face was set in deep lines of profound earnestness. He sifted and washed each word like a man panning for gold..."[3]*

Subsequently Sadhuji came to know the Lord in a full and real way. He also became free politically, for Nepal's King had been restored to power in 1951, overthrowing the Ranas who had ruled in Nepal over a hundred years and had imprisoned Sadhuji.

We had been in Darjeeling only three weeks when Sadhuji asked to share his testimony with the Nepali congregation before he returned to Nepal. We were mere novices in Nepali, so Millie promised to take notes for us.

Sadhuji walked up to the front of the church with his grey blanket slung over his shoulder. He began to speak in a quiet voice, a voice that commanded attention. Some men moved forward to hear him better. Others bent forward in their seats.

His opening words were simple, "I want to tell you what the Bible means to me. I don't want to lie at all. I want to tell only what I believe and what I have experienced."

He went on to tell of the great hunger there had been in his heart for such a long time, and of the tract that ultimately led to his believing in God.

"Some of the Buddhist teachings satisfied my intellect," he said, "but oh, my heart was not satisfied." Then he told of coming to Darjeeling and of his "friends" who had helped him.

---

[3] *World Vision* (a publication of WMPL, later renamed *Fellow Workers*) 1947.

"*My friends counseled me to pray to Jesus, even though I could not believe he was God. They counseled me to begin to read the Psalms that I might learn how to pray. The Psalms have become so precious to me! And then slowly–I cannot find words to describe how it happened. In fact, I don't know how it happened. I began to realize that Christ was no mere man, that He was more than man and if He was more than man, it meant that He was God. One thing that impressed me much was that every time in teaching others about the Holy Spirit or when I myself was thinking and studying, Christ always seemed to come to the foreground. He seemed to demand my attention. That caused me to think.*

"*It's a strange thing. I believe with all my heart in the Trinity and in Christ now, but how I came to believe, I cannot tell you. It was not through study. It was not through argument. Faith just came of itself. And I am not one to easily believe a thing. Just because someone teaches a thing, I cannot accept it or believe it. I must have a heart conviction that it is true. My study of the Buddhist Scriptures taught me that. But oh, I believe it now! There isn't a shade of doubt in my heart now.*

"*Do you know how it is with me these days? You know how it is after a person has been ill a long time and finally recovers and is well enough to go out-of-doors. He just marvels at all the beauties of nature which seem to stand forth in new and striking beauty and light. That is the way it is with me these days. My heart exults in Him. I feel as light as snow.*

"*Whether I walk on the road, or eat my meal, or talk with my friends, or pray, I am conscious of His presence with me every moment of the day. I **know** that He is with me. Christ reveals to us the loving kindness of God. He loved with a love that was not a human love. Human love is selfish. It only seeks something in return. It only loves that it may be loved in turn. Christ's love is not like that. Christ loves expecting nothing in return. He loves because He cannot help loving, for He is love.*"

Then he went on to read from 1 Peter 2:21 "For to this you were called, because Christ suffered for you, leaving you an example, that you should follow in his steps."

> *"If we begin to follow Christ, if we stand committed to preach His Gospel, it will necessarily involve suffering. But if Christ suffered for us, surely we should be willing to suffer for Him. We are to walk in His steps.*
>
> *"And so that is all I have to say. My long search for peace is ended. There is only peace and joy in my heart these days. The Bible ministers light and peace to me.*
>
> *"You must pray for me. I am going to return to my own country now. I need your prayer."*

Quietly Sadhuji took his seat and Pastor led in prayer for him.

Sadhuji's whole family came to St. Joseph's Mount for one last visit with us before leaving for Nepal. He sat sipping sweet Darjeeling tea as he said with great firmness, "Anyone can say 'I am the truth, the way,' but only Jesus can say 'I am the resurrection!'"

We all knelt together in prayer and committed our friend to the Lord. After Sadhuji returned to Kathmandu, he was very involved in politics. Later he was appointed a member of Parliament. Years later we were stunned to hear that he had died in a Kathmandu hospital of liver disease and pneumonia. We have no doubt that he is with the King of kings now and that we shall see him in his and our heavenly home.

What if no one had poked a tract through the prison bars to Sadhuji? Soon there would be many more life-giving messages to poke through the bars.

That Would Change

Millie Hasselquist and Becky Grimsrud, our senior missionaries, hadn't been in Darjeeling long when Jonathan Lindell, an experienced fellow missionary, gave some good advice for the two new recruits. "The best way to learn a language is to converse in it every day," he had counseled them. So Jonathan arranged for Millie to go to Auntie Ruth's house to talk with her for an hour a day.

Auntie Ruth lived with her brother, D. H. Mukhia, pastor of the Nepali St. Columba's Church in Darjeeling. The church had been built directly up the hill from the local Hindu temple and the Darjeeling railway station. The pastor's house was a small wooden structure perched behind the church.

On one of the first days Millie visited Auntie Ruth, the elderly Nepali lady burst into tears. Bit by bit Millie pieced together her story. "How can I find peace with God? I have committed so many sins! I have prayed and prayed and repented and repented, but how can I know I'm forgiven?" Auntie Ruth wiped the tears with a corner of her shawl.

Haltingly, searching for words in the new language, Millie pointed Auntie to Jesus, the Lamb of God. They read Bible promises together. Kneeling down beside Auntie's bed, they prayed together. The Holy Spirit helped Auntie Ruth to understand she needed to accept forgiveness, and that to continually plead for forgiveness was unbelief. Peace in ever deepening measure flowed into Auntie's heart. She became a confident, happy Christian.

Her fellowship was a tremendous boon to Millie and Becky, a real gift from the Lord. She helped them to understand which American customs, phrases or actions were hard for her people to understand and apt to be misconstrued. They studied the Bible together and prayed for the millions of Nepalis who did not know Jesus.

When Millie and Becky moved out to the village of Mirik, Auntie wanted to go along. They had no means to salary her as a worker, but they invited her to come along and share their home and food. They couldn't even promise pocket money for stamps. Yet she was happy to go along as a member of the team. Auntie Ruth was plucky and uncomplaining. She hiked up and down the hills as the three held classes in different Nepali homes. She never spoke of being tired.

They began each day at 6:30 with prayer. Reminiscing of those days, Millie wrote, "I cannot remember one ripple in the fellowship nor were any of us conscious of any adjustments to each other. We just fit together."

On cold winter evenings the three sat huddled around a smoky fireplace and a kerosene lamp. Becky and Millie spent much time in Bible study and reading. Auntie would read her Hindi Bible. She preferred it to the outdated Nepali translation. One evening she said, "How blessed you are! You have so many books in your language written about God! What treasures they contain! How strong you can become. We have so little. Sometimes I wish so much we had more!"

That would change! Becky and Millie later shared Auntie Ruth's longing with us. God would soon open the door for good Christian literature to be produced in Nepali. But first he needed to change us.

Good News from Africa

How they happened to come thousands of miles from Africa to Darjeeling we never knew. What they brought we'll never forget. A medical missionary from England to Rwanda, Dr. Joe Church, and his black African brother, William Nagenda, came to Darjeeling with wonderful news. We all gathered around to hear.

Nagenda and Church had been having continual revival in the work in Rwanda. They spoke very quietly and humbly. They didn't speak of the successes of their work but only of Jesus and His cleansing power. They told us that when we expect God to work we expect something dramatic to happen, as Naaman did.[4]

But God merely wants us to "go and wash," go to Jesus moment by moment and day by day for His continual cleansing. Our proud "stiff necks," as Brother William called them, must be continually bent so that Jesus can be our all in all. Jesus was so wonderfully precious to them. God did a deep work in Roy's and my hearts. We knew we needed the same walk with Jesus that they had.

When Brother William became ill, the two came to our home for two days to recuperate. They talked to us about the "openness and brokenness" that had so changed their lives. Roy and I both came to the place where we were willing to be "broken," willing to "bend our stiff necks" to Jesus and to one another. We opened up to each other confessing to one another sins that had hindered our fellowship with Jesus, sins of criticism, impatience, pride, and others. In cases where we had wrong attitudes toward others in the mission headquarters we confessed our sin first to Jesus and then to the person involved. What wonderful joy and cleansing came to our hearts when we experienced

---

[4] A Syrian army captain who went to the Israeli prophet Elisha to be healed. God's prophet told him "Go and wash yourself seven times in the Jordan." 2 Kings 5:10.

walking in the light with Jesus and with one another.

We learned a new chorus from Brother William:

Glory, glory hallelujah,
Glory, glory to the Lamb,
For the cleansing blood has reached me,
Glory glory to the Lamb.

Dr. Church said, "We have seven hundred men in Rwanda who have a similar testimony to brother Nagenda's. William's English was the best of all of them. That was the reason he was chosen for the trip."

The Nepali Christians noticed a tremendous change in our house. Jesus became more precious each new day. And now they were beginning to see the sweetness of walking in the light with Jesus and with one another. Four of the leaders of the local congregation got together, confessed their sins and asked one another for forgiveness. They were new people. Good news had come to Darjeeling.

However, we needed wheels capable of mountain driving to help us carry that good news to others.

At the Point of a Dagger

Clarence and Helen Hjelmervik and two little daughters were to move out to Mirik to live where Millie and Becky had begun a good work. Millie had gone on furlough after seven years in India. It was the common consensus that a jeep was essential for moving and obtaining household necessities. A jeep would be invaluable for visiting markets, holding clinics, and showing "magic lantern pictures" at night. Kerosene could be used for the cooking stove and for lanterns. Funds had already been provided for a vehicle.

An old US Army Willys jeep left over from World War II was being sold by Tashi, an entrepreneur Tibetan trader. Clarence Hjelmervik and Roy went off hiking twenty-eight miles to Kalimpong. They found a Nepali middle man, Bhim, to interpret from Tibetan into English and English into Tibetan.

Being an experienced mechanic, Clarence carefully examined the jeep. Bhim invited the men to his home. They sat around a low table.

A newspaper served as tablecloth. Tashi strode in, a broad-rimmed hat cocked over his right ear. A large turquoise earring dangled from his left ear, which he wore because he believed it would prevent him from being reincarnated as a donkey in the after life.

When Tashi saw Clarence and Roy, he bowed and stuck out his tongue as far as it would go—a Tibetan sign of respect!

The men sat cross-legged at the low table sipping tea. After half an hour of pleasantries Bhim queried, "Tashi, how much do you want for the jeep?"

"Six thousand rupees!" declared Tashi.

In true Asian bargaining custom, Roy countered, "Far too much! Make it three thousand!"

"No, no! Far too low" said Tashi, shaking his head. "Make it five thousand rupees!" "Four thousand" Roy countered. Back and forth they went.

Suddenly Tashi pulled out a short shiny dagger from a sheath hanging at his waist. Taking his dagger he reached across the table and drew the point straight down Roy' nose. Roy gasped, wondering if he had pushed Tashi too far.

"We'll cut it in half," Bhim translated Tashi's words. "Rupees four thousand, five hundred!"

Roy quickly agreed, offering a ride into Darjeeling. That settled the bargain. The four men got into the jeep to drive the twenty-eight miles back to Darjeeling where payment was to be arranged at the bank. Down the hill they drove, past tall bamboo trees. The road twisted back and forth, lower and lower until they crossed the narrow bridge over the rushing Tista River, close to sea level.

They began the long climb up seven thousand feet to Ghoom, a small market on the crest of the hill. Back and forth, higher and higher, the road climbed through groomed tea gardens. The air grew cooler.

Suddenly the engine sputtered and stopped. Lifting up the hood, Clarence began searching for the problem.

"The fan belt has broken!" he declared.

Being more familiar with mule trains, Tashi offered, "Let's push the jeep!"

Roy and Clarence took one look at the thousand foot climb still ahead of them and shook their heads. Tashi began groping under his belt inside of his trousers. After some effort, he pulled out the cord of his pajamas he was wearing underneath his pants and offered it as a substitute for the fan belt. Clarence deftly wrapped and tied the cord in place of the missing fan belt. The men climbed back in the jeep. The motor started and they were off. Another thousand feet further up they heaved a sigh of relief as the road crested at Ghoom.

After reaching Darjeeling, they shifted into low transfer to drive the steep climb up Mackintosh Road to St. Joseph's Mount.[5] They arrived just in time for supper. We invited Tashi and Bhim to our apartment. As we sat around the table, we were using soft plastic glasses for drinking water. Thinking these might be a novelty to Tashi, we explained through Bhim that these "glasses" would not break. Tashi grabbed his glass, got up from the table and hurled it down to the floor as hard as he could. To his delight it bounced all the way up to the fireplace mantel, unbroken. When it came time for dessert, we served red raspberry jello. As it jiggled on his spoon, he declared, "It's alive!"

That evening Tashi told us how China had declared that Tibet belonged to China and were sending in troops. Tashi wanted to perform a dance for us. He would soon be returning to Lhasa. Taking off his jacket and tying the long sleeves around his waist, he began a very heavy stomping dance in his high boots. The whole house shook. He sang a non-melodic sing-song tune that should have ended with "Long live Mao Tse Tong" but instead he sang, "**May He Soon Die!**"

We had acquired a jeep for the work, but we had also found memorable friends in Tashi and Bhim. Soon we would meet even more history-making unforgettable friends.

Nepal Border Fellowship Conference

Three months after arriving in Darjeeling we headed back to the plains to represent Darjeeling workers at the Nepal Border Fellowship Conference. Foreign missionaries were not yet allowed into Nepal. Little did we realize how close to a breakthrough in Nepali work we were!

---

[5] The old WWII jeep had a high set and a low set of gears popularly called "high transfer" and "low transfer." A short transfer lever was used to shift down to low transfer for especially steep or difficult terrain.

The train we took came to a jerking halt at 5 a.m. at Gorakhpur just south of the Nepal border. We had gone more than half way along Nepal's border west from Siliguri and Darjeeling. The plains people were already astir. After bargaining with the owner, we started off in a horse-drawn cart for the Gorakhpur Bible School. Soon we were greeted at the door of the school by white-haired founder and director, Mr. A. Garrison.

While still a student at a New York Missionary Training Institute, Mr. Garrison received a call to work in India and Nepal. On coming to India, he was assigned to work in South India and labored there for forty years. Now nearly seventy, when most folk think of retirement, he and his wife had moved to hot, dusty, malaria-infested Gorakhpur. They had given themselves to training Nepalis to minister to their own people just north of them and were beginning to learn Nepali.

First begun in 1935, the Nepal Border Fellowship met there in conference from March 28-31, 1952. We soon forgot the blistering heat and dusty roads as we fellowshipped with those of our common calling. From Nepal's western, eastern, and southern borders came nearly twenty-five folk representing Lutherans, Presbyterians, Baptists, and Pentecostals. Ten different missions met together, all praying for an opportunity to work in Nepal to communicate the Gospel. From south India came three young men who each felt called by God to bring the good news of Jesus to

Prayer took priority at the conference. We began and ended the day with intercession for the land so long closed to the Gospel. Mr. Garrison spoke on the theme of fellowship. We saw afresh our common salvation and fellowship in Christ and with each other, regardless of our different denominational backgrounds. Christ partook of our nature that we in turn might share His. God had planned the deepest fellowship for us who were members of Christ. We found the depth of this fellowship with Christ through suffering with Him.

As we shared together our common vision and opportunities for work, one thing stood out crystal clear: our main task was to train and equip Spirit-filled Nepali Christians to witness for their Master in their own homeland. In 1951 there had been a revolution in Nepal restoring the rightful King Tribhuvan to power. Christian Nepalis could finally go in and reveal Christ in word and deed though they would need to withstand persecution. This was a tremendous opening. We would need to train them and equip them with good literature and visual aids.

We were encouraged.

The day after the conference, British Dr. Lily O'Hanlon, better known as Pat, and Irish Hilda Steele invited us to their home and medical work in Nautanwa, right on the Nepal border. After a slow three-hour train ride we arrived in Nautanwa. Walking down the roads our feet sank into flour-like dust. Sullen eyes followed us. The houses were made of mud with steep slanting thatch roofs and bamboo frames.

Soon many began calling out, "*Salaam Memsahib! Salaam Memsahib!*"[6] Obviously Pat and Hilda were well known and much appreciated. Their home, just a short distance from the railway station, was an ideal location to meet many Nepalis who came over the border to visit India.

That evening I tagged along behind Hilda as she visited a number of patients. One young boy, paralyzed from tetanus (lock jaw), lay on a string-bed. We made numerous visits into tiny mud huts, the entrances so low we had to virtually crawl to get in. What darkness inside, physically and spiritually!

Later we gathered in the local square for a Gospel meeting. The believers sang a Nepali hymn in a rousing Nepali tune. Their leader, David Mukhia, gave a simple message on the Living God, Jesus Christ. Standing nearby was a very antagonistic local Indian. He tried to interrupt and distract the listeners, but whenever he started, we began singing hymns and bound Satan's work in him. Finally the fellow sat down quietly and listened attentively.

At 7 the next morning we met with the Nepali believers in a thatch hut. We all sat on grass mats. After a few hymns one of the believers led in Bible Study. His face shone with the joy of the Lord. Then we went back to Pat and Hilda's for breakfast.

Village folk had been coming to the dispensary since 6 a.m. By the time the doors were opened, there was quite a crowd. David's wife, Premi, took out a roll of Bible story pictures and told the story of Jesus to the whole group while the patients waited for treatment. She told how Jesus healed sickness, forgave sins and gave eternal life. The sick listened attentively. One old soul who had walked two days to come to the dispensary plunked herself right down in front of Premi. It was obviously the first time she had heard the story of Jesus. Then Pat

---

[6] Hello Madam Sahib. *Sahib* was a title of respect for a European in Colonial India, later for any male. It was adapted to form Memsahib as a title of respect for women.

began seeing the patients. They came with eye infections, aches, pains, leprosy and open sores. She wrote out prescriptions, and Hilda doled out the medicine.

That evening I asked Hilda to tell us her story.

"I was trained in poultry raising and market gardening." she began. "I was working for an inveterate gambler. My mother thought that wasn't good, so she insisted I change my job. Then I went to look after the poultry on the farm of Mr. & Mrs. Strong. You know their son Trevor and his wife Patricia are doctors at the Mission Hospital in Raxaul, right on the Nepal border.

"I was a hard drinker and heavy smoker at that time. When Mr. Strong offered to buy me some cigarettes on the next trip to the village, even though he disapproved of my

Back row: Dr. "Pat" O'Hanlon, Alma, Joan Short. In front, Hilda Steele and Jean Raddon at the Nepal Border Fellowship Conference, 1952.

smoking, I thought 'these people are different.'

"I began to read the Bible, and seeing the Strongs' commitment, I gave my heart to the Lord. One day while in one of the chicken houses I felt a very strong call to the mission field. I took missionary training and then came to India with the Zenana Bible and Medical Missions. That was in 1932, just after you were born. I hadn't been out long when I developed eye trouble and TB. I had to return to Ireland and was told I didn't have long to live! But the Lord touched me and I made a speedy recovery.

"Meanwhile I met Pat and we both felt God calling us to Nepali work. When I came back to India we took over Dr. Kitty Harbord's work here in Nautanwa. We have been waiting nearly twenty years for the door to open!"

I marveled at their patience and wondered how long it would be before Nepal's door fully opened.

Our train back to Gorakhpur left at noon. Three of the Christian Nepali men sat in the train for an hour saving our seats for us. Because there was to be a mela or country fair down the railway line, the train was crammed with people. Our compartment was designed to seat sixteen. I counted fifty. The local folk sat on the roof, hung out the doors, and clung to the windows outside the train. How grateful we were for our friends!

Enroute back to Siliguri and Darjeeling we took a side trip to Raxaul, the railhead that led to the only road leading directly to Kathmandu. Hundreds of Nepalis flocked into India at Raxaul. Some came on religious pilgrimages, others for schooling in India, some for trade or to seek employment in tea estates. The famous Gurkha Nepali soldiers often entered India via Raxaul.[7]

Dr. Cecil Duncan, son of the Scottish Presbyterian Duncans of Darjeeling, had built a hospital in Raxaul in 1930. Many Nepalis came there for treatment. The hospital was closed during World War II. Then a rare medical team, Trevor and Patricia Strong, had come from Ireland and reopened the hospital in 1948. They welcomed us warmly and took

---

[7] Nepalis were called "Gurkha" or in Nepali "Gurkhali" because King Prithwi Narayan Shah, who unified Nepal into one kingdom in 1769 AD, came from Gorkha in central Nepal between Pokhara and Kathmandu.

us on a complete tour of their medically and spiritually far-reaching ministry. It was like finding an oasis.

We were so thankful to get back to Darjeeling to find our little men well and happy in Dan Mit's good care. By contrast to the dusty plains, Darjeeling seemed so clean. The air was fresh and crisp. There

Paul cared for by Dan Mit.

were no mosquitoes or cobra snakes. We were grateful to be living at such a refreshing altitude and among people known for their cheerfulness.

The Nepal Border Fellowship Conference had shown us how many people had been working and waiting for Nepal to open to the Gospel. Now that it was possible for Nepali Christians to enter the country, we came home with a clear vision to train and equip Nepalis to take the Gospel to their own people.

The possibility of Nepal's door opening to missionaries came sooner than any of us anticipated.

History in a Brown Envelope

Three months later, Pat and Hilda came to spend a month's vacation with us in Darjeeling, away from the grueling heat of the plains. Pat brought along a large registered envelope that had been duly closed with conspicuous red wax seals. Her eyes sparkled with joy as she shared the contents. The Nepal government had granted permission to open a hospital in Pokhara, six days walk west of Kathmandu. It was the first time Protestant missions had been given permission to work within the borders of Nepal. We burst into thanksgiving and praise to God as we heard the wonderful news.

"There are restrictions," Pat read. "We are not to meddle in politics. We are not to 'proselytize' and we are to only worship our God within the walls of our premises."

Nepal's door had finally begun to open. We lingered after dinner that memorable day.

"Are there any roads to Pokhara?" Roy queried.

"Not a one. No wheeled vehicles of any kind. Everything we'll need for building a hospital, from cement and pipes to an operating table and bandages must all be carried in on coolie backs or be flown in by airplane," Pat responded, pressing her lips together with determination.

"And the planes fly only when the weather is decent!" Hilda added, looking out the window at the monsoon clouds surrounding St. Joseph's Mount.

"There's no electricity, no running water, no window glass," she added thoughtfully.

"There are no communications out of Pokhara. Mail won't reach us for weeks at a time," Pat mused.

"But Nepal has no postal system. How can we reach you by mail?" I asked.

"Through the British Embassy in Kathmandu," Pat replied.

Our minds spun with questions. "How can we help? What can women in the homeland do?" I asked, thinking of the caring ladies in our church family.

"They can sew surgical gowns and roll bandages out of old sheets," Hilda declared.

Before the dishes were cleared off the table we paused to praise

God. Once again He had answered the prayer of countless intercessors around the world. He had promised to supply all that was needed. He would be faithful. After so long a wait, He had opened the door. But we still needed a Bible training center in a village setting so many Nepalis from India could be equipped to also slip through that open door.

Chapter 3

Village Roots

Angelic Props

Pat and Hilda's good news and that open door spurred our WMPL team on to train Nepalis. Roy and Clarence Hjelmervik were teaching evening Bible classes in Darjeeling. Most people in Nepal lived in villages without electricity. We thought that a Nepali village without modern conveniences would be a much simpler, better context to prepare Nepalis to go into their ancestral homeland than a westernized city like Darjeeling. We all felt it was time to expand the work into the "nearby" village of Mirik.

Fran Swenson had come to join Becky who was alone with Auntie Ruth. The Hjelmerviks would move first. We would follow after we completed our first year of language study.

Clarence and Helen packed their basic belongings into the jeep along with their little blond daughters Lois and Carna. We committed them into God's care and they started off.

The road to Mirik was at first tarred, leading through a beautiful forest area. But as it turned south at Semana (meaning border) it became a narrow dirt road cut into the hillside. The steep road zigzagged back and forth, down, down from 6,000 feet to 4,000 feet and then up again to an elevation of 5,000 feet.

Along the dirt road sat poor Nepali women breaking piles of stones. We could hear the K-chink, K-chink, as they hammered larger stones into gravel for the road surface.

At one point the road climbed about one foot in every four. As the jeep started up the short hill, Clarence began to shift into another set of gears, from high transfer into low transfer. The wheels began spinning and losing traction on the slippery clay. There was no gravel on this stretch. Suddenly the jeep slipped to the edge of the road, ending at a precarious 30 degree angle on the edge of a treacherous, steep slope to the valley below. Cautiously the whole family crawled out. Little Lois and Carna clung to their Mommy.

Did angels prop up the jeep and keep it from tipping over? It seemed so.

While Clarence and Helen praised God profusely for protection, two land rovers full of passengers stopped to help. Unloading some of the baggage they eased the jeep back up onto the road. The men pushed as Clarence drove up that steep stretch. Soon the travelers had all the belongings up the hill and back in the jeep. The little family proceeded on their way.

But that wasn't the end of that day's excitement. The family moved into the stone and mud-walled house called *Chatra Niwas*, the Nepali name for "student residence," that Becky had rented for them. When they were getting ready for bed, Clarence heard a piercing meow outside the house. Shining his flashlight out the back door he spied a leopard slinking away, leaving a dead cat behind.

This new program was not to begin easily. It called for serious spiritual warfare. However, they were not alone in this battle. There were more surprising things to happen, but Jesus promised, "I am with you always, to the very end of the age," (Matthew 28:20).

Saved from Lightning

When the African friends from Rwanda came to Darjeeling with their word of openness and brokenness, some of the believers shared the message with Shilling. He took it all deep into his soul. While he lay under the regulation red wool blankets of the tuberculosis sanatorium, he recalled individuals whom he had wronged in bygone days. He wrote clear-cut letters, asking forgiveness and expressing the change Christ had brought in his life.

It was a miraculous day for Shilling when the doctor gave him a discharge from the sanatorium with instructions to rest and report back in three months. It was the summer of 1952.

Even though the burden for his two young sons living with his parents lay heavily on his heart, he felt compelled by the Lord to accept Hjelmervik's invitation to rest and recuperate in their home in Mirik.

Later Clarence wrote about Shilling:

"He is following a definite program of Scripture memorization so that he might be 'ready always to give an answer to every man'. All reports that we have received of him have been an honor to the Lord, from Hindus as well as church members. His whole purpose in life is to preach the Gospel."

Mirik lay submerged in darkness. The lilting sound of flutes on distant hills had faded into night. Miniature oil lamps had been blown out and the village lay in slumber. Suddenly a jagged bolt of lightning stabbed the sky and struck the crest of the hill. It flashed down the tin roof and mud wall of the missionary home, burning a hole in papers lying in the broad windowsill inches from Shilling's bed. He awoke dazed, realizing how miraculously he had been spared. God had a good purpose for his life.

In October, during Hindu festival holidays, we held a Youth Conference at St. Joseph's Mount. About twenty Nepali Christians trudged up the steep road every day for seven days to consider the missionary challenge of Nepal.

Shilling and Clarence came back to Darjeeling for the Conference. "Not I but Christ," was Shilling's topic the first evening, and he had everyone's attention as he spoke. "If we follow 'Not I but Christ,' how soon we grow spiritually. For a long time I didn't know this and was spiritually low, but when I discovered this truth, and used it, I could praise the Lord."

Then Pastor D.H. Mukhia spoke, "The Lord has been speaking to me these days and showing me that if I am not willing to go to Nepal with the Gospel myself, I cannot expect others to offer themselves to go."

Roy and Clarence took turns teaching on revival and walking in the light with one another. Five gave their lives to full time service for the Lord, including Kamala Thapa and Indira Pradhan. They were learning the full meaning of walking with Jesus in obedience and abandonment to Him.

The Nepalis in Darjeeling had yearned for the proclamation of the Gospel in their homeland of Nepal for years. Ganga Prasad Pradhan, the second Nepali convert in the Darjeeling Nepali Church, baptized in 1875, had composed a folk song which plaintively voiced their feelings. This song has been sung by Nepali Christians in India for more than two generations.

The song starts out with *Prabhu, arji sunniliao!*[8]

O Lord, hear our prayer,
Open the door of salvation for the Gurkhalis.
Father, Son, Holy Spirit, hear our petition.
Show us the way by a cloudy, fiery pillar,
Peoples of different regions are to east, west and south;
Tibet is north, and Nepal our home is in the middle
There are cities: Thapathali, Bhatgaon, Patan, Kathmandu;
Our desire is to make them your devotees.
Up, brothers! We must go, ignoring hate and shame,
    Leaving wealth, people, comfort,
    to do the holy task in that land.

After the Conference, Shilling went back to the sanatorium for a checkup. The TB specialist, Dr. Michael, had just returned from further training in Denmark. On examining Shilling he looked him square in the eye and said, "You should never have been discharged. Both of your lungs are infected with TB. You must have absolute bed rest!" came his verdict. Shilling's shoulders sagged. He was numb with disappointment. "If you stay flat in bed for three to six months, we will have part of one lung collapsed and you will be back doing normal work," he added.

Because there was no vacancy in the sanatorium for Shilling, we WMPLers offered him an isolated sun porch in St. Joseph's Mount. He could have his own dishes, bathroom and complete bed rest. So the sun porch was prepared and Shilling tumbled into bed. He was a great boon to our language learning as we chatted through the window. He began to call Roy and me *"Bajay and Boju"* which translated from Nepali means "Grandfather and Grandmother." But these are also the terms used for a priest and his wife.

After six months flew by, Shilling had a bed reserved in Madar TB Sanatorium far away in Ajmir, in western India. There he had six ribs removed and a lung collapsed.[9]

_____

[8] Lord, hear our prayer.

[9] Such severe TB was treated by "plombage," collapsing the lung to close infected cavities and stop the TB bacilli from spreading.

He used even that experience for a testimony to the Lord:

> *"If I had counted the ribs very dear and had not been willing to give them up, I would have died in the long run. But I was willing to surrender them, and as a result, I found new life. So it is in our spiritual life. If I hold one thing as dear unto myself, it will mean spiritual death in the end, whereas if I'm willing to give it up to Jesus, then I could find new life."*

Shilling had indeed found new life, but that was only the beginning. God was going to move him into an even greater witness.

A Moving Experience

We could hardly wait to rip open the envelope containing our language exam results. Fifty percent was passing. We both got seventy-one. Roy's points were all in grammar and composition, mine in conversation and reading. We truly complemented one another.

Dr. and Mrs. Frank Laubach, the worldwide literacy experts of "Each one teach one," visited us in Darjeeling. Known as the "Apostle to illiterates," Dr. Laubach invited Roy: "Come with me to Nepal."

"I would love to go. We can improve the national literacy rate from 2 percent," Roy replied. "But I would rather send Nepalis who really know the language." He then arranged for two top Nepali educators to accompany Dr. Laubach to Nepal. To the amazement of those educators, Dr. Laubach, nearly seventy years old, worked tirelessly. Those "Laubach" literacy charts were completed in a short time, but it took the Nepal government a long time to print them.

The day finally came when our Hagen family was to move to rural Mirik. Our four-year-old future mechanical engineer David took seriously the logistics of the move. "Les go to Mirik and take potty!"

Clarence and Roy had built a trailer for the jeep to accommodate our move. But the equipment needed to add brakes to the trailer was not to be had in Darjeeling, so we were doubly cast on the Lord for His goodness and protection. We loaded household basics for our family of four in the jeep and trailer and we were off. God graciously helped us the entire journey, even on the steepest hill. Soon we were winding our way through Mirik's large Thurbo Tea Estate and hills of neatly terraced tea bushes. Just past the large factory we came to Mirik's doughnut-shaped *bazaar* (market) with a post office and shops for rice, spices and kitchen basics. Beyond the market, terraced corn fields and simple village homes covered the large part of Mirik that wasn't used for growing tea.

As we drove past the market—or bazaar, as everyone called it—we glimpsed the Himalayas vaulting high into the sky. We saw a pine forest in the opposite direction, and, wonder of wonders, a flat area large enough for a soccer field.

Becky had made arrangements for us to rent a little house quite near the market. Large stones stuck together with mud and then whitewashed formed the eighteen inch thick walls of the five-room house. Three rooms were 10 feet by 8 feet, two rooms 6 feet by 6 feet. Two of the larger rooms would be bedrooms; the center room would have an iron stove, cupboard, table and two cane chairs for visitors. The two tiny rooms 6 feet by 6 feet would be for a guest bedroom and for Roy's office. The house contained no shelves or closets before our arrival. The roof was made of corrugated tin. From the front of our little home we had a wonderful view of the "snows," the beautiful Himalayas.

David was right in his thoughtful planning for the potty because there was no bathroom and no toilet. Previous residents had just gone out in the field, or behind corn stalks or a tree. So the latrine was the first thing to be built after we moved in.

During the three-month monsoon season we would have "running" water with about 200 inches of rain between mid-June and mid-September. A large 55-gallon drum sat outside one corner of our stone and mud house underneath the downspout. The rain ran off the roof. We ran to get it. Then we ran to throw it out!

We joked about "dry rain" and "wet rain." "Dry rain" fell when you used an umbrella and stayed dry. "Wet rain" came through the umbrella! Besides, we didn't get *that* much rain. Cherripungi to our east had four hundred inches (ten meters) of rain per year!

The rest of the year was very dry. *Maili*, our household help, would carry a four-gallon kerosene tin of water up from a spring far below the house. The tin was held on her back by a *namlo* or rope slung over her forehead and around the tin.

Rose and gardenia bushes decorated the front corners of the mud structure. An Aladdin lamp, small kerosene lamps, candles and flashlights were our sources of light. We washed clothes on a scrub board and ironed with a sadiron. I had purchased it from an antique dealer in the States who had been surprised that I planned to use it!

Just a few yards from our home was a wooden cookhouse with an earthen floor. It too had a corrugated roof, but wooden walls. That little building would have a very important place in the future work in Mirik.

A ten-minute walk between corn fields on one side and pine trees on the other led to Gurung Cottage. Becky and Auntie Ruth lived there. That was where we would begin the Bible School for Nepalis to be taught in their own Nepali language.

Starting the Bible School was something like climbing Mount Everest. We were working to move a mountain by faith.

Everest Conquered

Everyone in Mirik knew about mountain-climber Tenzing Norgay. The Nepalis declared he had three lungs. But we knew him as a jolly Sherpa who routinely wore tan jodhpurs, red wool knee-high socks, a brown jacket and a visor cap.

Born in northeast Nepal, he was one of fourteen children, eight of whom died at childbirth. Though he was illiterate, he could communicate in thirteen different languages, including French, Italian, and Japanese. But it was always in English that he greeted, us as though he had found long-lost friends. His home was just a short distance from where we had lived in Darjeeling.

Sherpas are known for their skill in guiding Himalayan mountain climbers. Tenzing had been on six previous Everest expeditions. When asked "Why do you want to climb Everest?" he casually replied, "Because it is there."

We were just settling into our new home in Mirik when Tenzing and Edmund Hillary, a New Zealand beekeeper, made world news right in our "back yard." Eighty miles northwest of us as the crow flies, they together reached the summit of Everest on May 23, 1953. The two vowed to one another never to reveal which one of them really reached the summit first.

After his conquest of Everest, Tenzing built a mountaineering institute in Darjeeling, where one day our son Paul would take mountain climbing lessons. Years later we would spend a week with Tenzing on the roof of the world in Tibet, where he served as a very knowledgeable tour guide and an interesting roommate for our son Karl.

Tenzing Norgay is showing Roy the key to the Potala in Lhasa, Tibet.

Though he was a world-famous mountain climber, Tenzing knew what we were experiencing in village life.

Village Life

Village life in Mirik was very different from city life in Darjeeling. *Maili*, who carried water for us, also washed clothes by hand. If the sun shone we hung clothes on a line, but if it rained we draped them over an igloo-shaped bamboo frame positioned over a pan of hot charcoal. The charcoal gave off fumes and smoke which often made the clothes yellow. Keeping the door open for fresh air was essential when we dried indoors.

Another Nepali, *Bahadur*, did our grocery shopping. He bought rice, lentils, potatoes, onions and spices. Fresh vegetables and meat were usually available only on Sundays when farmers brought their produce to Mirik bazaar. Bahadur cooked over a small coffee-can-size stove of charcoal. On Mondays we got out the pressure cooker and canned the meat purchased on Sundays to provide meat for the rest of the week.

A network of narrow, winding footpaths led to and past our home. We were right in the middle of terraced cornfields, ten minutes' walk away from the only auto road and fifteen minutes from the bazaar and the post office.

Roy soon hired a local high school teacher to continue his second year of language study. Mornings I home schooled David and Paul.

Three months after moving to Mirik our family went back to St. Joseph's Mount, anticipating our next baby's arrival. Santal missionary Alice Axelson was on hand to care for David and Paul. At 2 a.m. on September 15, 1953, I awoke realizing, "This is the day!" Roy walked with me a mile down the hill to a British midwife's home. She answered our knock at 4 a.m. with, "Dith a minute. Wait till I put in my deeth and wath my hands." Kenneth Christy arrived twenty minutes later. We were so thankful for another healthy little fellow.

Back in Mirik many of our Nepali neighbors came to see the new

Bahadur preparing a charcoal fire for cooking Hagen family meals outside the cookhouse that was used for the printing press.

baby. They looked shocked. "Can he see?" they asked. They had never seen a baby with beautiful blue eyes. They had only seen brown Nepali eyes or the milky-blue eyes of the blind. We happily assured them that Kenny could see.

As the untreated floor boards in our home gradually dried out, the cracks between them grew wider and wider. Our little men were adept at dropping silverware through the cracks. Finally our cutlery supply ran so low that Roy had to pull up some boards and lower David down to the crawl level to recover much needed spoons and forks.

Our WMPL family in Mirik was growing. Fran Swenson, Betty Hanson, Ruth Overvold and Herman Simrose were all hard at language study. All four would have future ministry in Nepal.

Roy carefully prepared a syllabus for the Bible school, never dreaming that our own little hazel-eyed Paul would one day teach there. We prayed much for wisdom and God's plan for the school, as well as for those who would attend.

But opposition was brewing to our being in Mirik and preparing to start a Bible school.

Black Sealing Wax

What were these three registered letters at the Mirik post office, all sealed with ominous-looking black sealing wax? Roy had just signed to receive all three. One letter was for us, one for Becky at Gurung Cottage and one for the Hjelmerviks in the other house. What could those letters contain?

Roy cautiously opened the envelope and read the eviction order from our landlords:

"We have been ordered to appear in the Darjeeling Kutchery (Courthouse) for renting houses to foreigners. We are threatened with losing all our property. Please vacate the three houses within thirty days."

God had sent us to Mirik. We had obeyed. The work was His. Now He would have to keep us there. We were totally cast upon the Lord, as we fasted and prayed.

We took courage from Psalm 105:12-14: "When they were but few in number, and strangers in it . . . He allowed no one to oppress them." We also claimed Isa.54:17: "No weapon forged against you will prevail, and you will refute every tongue that accuses you. This is the heritage of the servants of the Lord, and this their vindication from me."

A little card someone had sent me gave great encouragement:

> *Fret not,*
> *He loves thee. John 13:9*
> *Faint not,*
> *He holds thee. Psalm 139:10*
> *Fear not,*
> *He keeps thee. Psalm 121:3*

Then a second letter came from our landlords:

> *"We have found it wiser to apply for permits to rent our houses to the World Mission Prayer League."*

The permits were eventually granted. What a relief that we didn't have to move! We praised and gave thanks.

> *"He causes us to dwell in safety." Psalm 4:8*

Unknown to us, God had already been preparing students to come to the Bible school.

The Well-Thumbed Book

Purna Maya Thapa, better known as "Kamala's mother," was one of the first to attend the Bible school that Roy was beginning in Gurung Cottage.

There had been so many things for her to worship—the images sitting on the god shelf in her home and in the Hindu temple, as well as the sun, moon, stars, trees and stones. For ten-to-twenty weeks each year she and her family fasted Tuesdays and Saturdays, drinking only water. Every new moon and full moon were fast days too. They believed God was in the sun, moon, stars, rivers and stones which they worshiped.

The religious regulations for a teacher of Hindus, such as Kamala's mother, forbad her to eat beef or buffalo meat. This Thapa family was part of a Nepali ethnic group called Magars. The only meat that Magars were allowed to eat was pork, mutton, or goat.

Kamala's mother found it difficult to be the second wife of a Gurkha army officer who drank heavily. There was continual quarreling. One day her husband stormed, "I'm leaving. From now on the children are your responsibility!" Bundling up a few basics, he stalked out of the house.

Kamala's mother's black hair was always neatly combed into a large bun worn low on her neck. Soon she became known in Mirik as a leading Hindu devotee. "We must build a temple here in Mirik" she declared. Contributions were collected. "I'll order an image from Manipur where I used to live. I know the maker of images there." When the day came for the official opening of the temple, she could barely peer over the many flower garlands honoring her.

Her oldest son chose a military career. Her next son, Tej Bahadur, or *Maila*, meaning second son, enrolled in the local Scots Mission grade school. Maila studied the Bible and a little Christian teaching, just enough to pass the examinations. His mother warned him, "If the Christian teacher touches you when you have some food in your pocket, you **must** throw it out."

One day Maila had a pocket full of dry corn and soybeans he liked to nibble on. His class lined up to march into school, but Maila took a step out of line. The teacher touched his shoulder, reminding him to get into line. Maila reluctantly threw out all his precious snacks.

In 1950, unbelievably torrential rains devastated the Darjeeling District. Twenty-four inches fell within forty-eight hours. Crops were destroyed, roads were washed out, and food became scarce.

Then Kamala became very sick. Her mother called in the witch doctor, but no amount of chanting, drumming or offerings brought any improvement. Kamala lay ill on her wooden bed, hot with fever. Finally in desperation, her mother said, "I'm going to call the foreign nurse." Giving a slight cough outside Becky's door, she waited for someone to answer. Becky opened the door. "Come in, come in!"

"Please, Missahib, come see my daughter. She is very sick. Her body is hot and she doesn't want to eat anything."

With a sideward tilt of her head, Becky agreed and gathered up some medicine. She and Auntie Ruth walked down the slippery red-clay path, as Kamala's mother padded politely behind them, directing them through the cornfields.

The house had only two rooms and a verandah. The walls were of bamboo covered with mud, the floor of mud mixed with manure to make the mud firm. Though it was made of mud, it was amazingly clean. The room where Kamala lay was full of hard wooden beds.

While Becky treated Kamala, Auntie Ruth invited Kamala's mother to a mother's Bible class at Gurung Cottage. Becky visited daily until Kamala had completely recovered from typhoid fever. Kamala's mother came to the Friday mother's meeting. She came faithfully. She listened earnestly and intently. Her faith grew. Then one day before Millie left for a furlough, Kamala's mother told them that she believed in Jesus. She began to pour out her heart. By writing her story, Millie gave her voice.[10]

> "*'Ever since I was a little girl, I have had a great desire in my heart to know God. How I was to find Him I didn't know. I did everything the Hindu scriptures told me. I fasted. I offered sacrifices. I called the priests in. But nothing brought peace to my heart. Nothing satisfied that thirst within.*
>
> "*'When I was a little girl, I went to a mission school for four months. Every day we used to sing, and I was given a little song book.'*
>
> "*She arose, went inside, and returned with a little book, well thumbed and worn, – so well worn, in fact, that many of the sheets had no margins left at all! She began to turn over the pages as she continued her story.*
>
> "*'I loved these songs. There was something about them that brought peace to my heart. My favorite was this.' Her searching fingers had found the right page and she began to sing,*

---

[10] M. Hasselquist, *World Vision*, Dec. pp 17-20, 1953.

"'Lord Jesus Christ, to Thee I fly,
Unless Thou help me, I must die.
And take me as I am,
My only plea, Thou diedst for me,
So take me as I am.

"And then she continued, 'I couldn't remember the tune
for some of these, but I used to sing them anyway, making up
my own. Whenever my heart was especially heavy, I would
take this little book and sit down and sing, and somehow it
helped.
"'And then you came. About six months before that, I
had given up my fasting. It yielded no peace. I was almost
through with all Hinduism. I knew that my own religion did
not satisfy my heart. Then you came and invited me to your
home. At the first meeting in your house, when I heard about
Jesus, there was a fierce struggle in my heart for a while. I
knew that this was what I was seeking, and yet there was a
storm within. But only for a while. Then I gave in, and peace
came, and I knew that day that I had found what I had been
seeking.'"

Her life changed completely. She became happy and patient, sang
new songs and read her Bible faithfully. Her second son, Maila,
couldn't help noticing the tremendous change in his mother. "How
awful," he thought, "that she should become a Christian, worse than
the lowest of all Hindu castes." But one day, he too, would change, but
only after the blood ran.

The Blood Ran

"What to do? What to do?" Maila said to himself.

"I can live a good life and obtain salvation! But my mother and the
Bible woman Ruth are saying that there is no other way to get salvation
but through Jesus! I'm going to see my Dad. The *Gita*[11] says it is
wrong to change our religion. And that is just what my mother has
done!"

---

[11] *Gita* is short for the Hindu scriptures *Bhagavadgita*.

Then Nepal's Door Opened

Maila had only been on the hot plains a short while when he fell sick and headed right back to Mirik. Then he became violently ill with malaria. Some Nepali Christians came to visit him, along with Roy. Roy said to him, "Maila, pray to Jesus. He's alive. He hears you."

"Mother keeps saying, 'If you pray to Jesus and confess your sins, Jesus will heal you,'" he replied. He had already fainted a number of times that day. That evening after everyone was in bed, Maila prayed, "If you are the true God, please heal me!" That night he slept well. He had no more fever.

"Who healed me? My Hindu god or the Christian God?" A great conflict filled Maila's mind. A strong wind blew the nearby bamboo trees till they bent low. Maila feared their mud-covered bamboo home would collapse. Maila prayed, "If you are the true God, make the wind stop blowing!" The wind stopped immediately. The next day rain fell in sheets. Again Maila prayed, "If you are the true God, let the moon shine tonight!" The rain stopped. That evening the hills lay bathed in moonlight. Then Maila prayed his fourth prayer, "If you are the true God, let it rain tonight." It rained.

Finally Maila was assured that Jesus was the true God. He confessed his sins and said to his mother, "I want to follow Christ." Then he prayed, "You are the true God. I confess my sins. I believe

Jonathan Thapa became a good writer and press manager.

54

that Jesus died on the cross for my sins."

There was a slight cough outside our front door, the Nepali way of knocking. Maila came to tell Roy of his answers to prayer and his decision to follow Jesus.

Later Maila felt proudly, "Because I have accepted Jesus, Jesus has given me salvation." He still had much to learn, including that nothing we do gives us salvation.

Some months later he had been out witnessing about how Jesus had suffered for him. That night after everyone was asleep, he was up reading the Bible.

A drunk came lumbering down the path toward their home and yelled out terrible insults to his mother. Maila became very angry, went out and hit the fellow until the blood ran, and then left him by the path. When he went back into the house, he began to think that perhaps he had killed the man. He realized how sinful and awful his own heart was. He wept and wept. His mother awakened and tried to console him. Midst tears of remorse he confessed his sin and realized fully that Jesus alone had saved him, that nothing of his own merit could bring salvation.

The next day the drunk and one of his buddies came to Maila's home. "I'm going to report you to the police" he thundered. Maila admitted his wrong and asked for forgiveness, whereupon the drunk forgave him.

Before he was baptized, he studied four months in the Bible school. Then at his baptism he took the name Jonathan (Thapa). Jonathan was indeed a true friend of Jesus, as he gave his brilliant gift of writing to the whole Nepali-speaking world.

Barefoot Teacher

No one knew what God had in store for Manu. She had wanted to become a Christian, had come to Bible studies at Becky's, and had been baptized. But then her family rejected her; and she had faced that closed door.

Manu, a simple, eighteen-year-old, primary school teacher, came barefoot three and a half miles from a tea-estate village to the Sunday service at Mirik. At her baptism on the same day as Kamala's mother's baptism, Manu chose "Martha" as her Christian name. Kamala's mother chose "Miriam."

She had only been a Christian a short while when she sat huddled in front of our tiny iron stove. The light of the fire flickered through the open grate onto Manu's soft face and shiny black hair. To follow Jesus meant to love Him above all else, to walk in His ways and to trust Him for life's details.

She gazed at the fire, as her almond-shaped eyes narrowed. She had a good teaching position. Should she quit and go to Bible school? It meant forsaking a secure job and stepping out in faith that God would supply her daily needs. That was a whole new concept.

She lifted her head. Her eyes fell on a little blue and silver plaque on the wall that read, "He will silently plan for you!"

That settled it. "Yes, I'll go to Bible school!" she said.

She wrote her Christian friend, Alice Rai, whom she had known in Teacher Training School in Kalimpong, encouraging her to attend Bible school too.

The barefoot teacher, Mansubba Rai.

Alice replied, "Yes, I'll come."

They would be two of the first five students to attend the first year of the Bible school. The Lord was preparing His students.

Sometime later a Nepal Border Fellowship Conference was held in Darjeeling.

During the conference, Auntie Ruth stood up to speak. She told how Pat and Hilda, who had been the first Protestant missionaries to go to Nepal, had invited her to Nepal, saying "Come to Pokhara! We need Christian Nepali midwives here!"

Auntie replied, "I'm 65, but I'll go."

She and another Nepali nurse took the long train journey to Nautanwa, Pat and Hilda's original base. It was during the monsoons. She said,

> *"We walked six miles and waded through two rivers to reach the grassy airfield for a plane to Pokhara. When the plane didn't show up, we had to walk back again. We did this six days in a row. We nearly gave up, but God answers prayer and on the seventh day the plane arrived. In two hours we were safely in Pokhara.*
>
> *"I worked there six months. The medical opportunities are numerous. The roads are mere paths, straight up and straight down. The people there know nothing of Jesus.*

> *"We Nepalis must teach our own people about Jesus. The Mis-sahibs are not allowed to preach. You are young. I am old. Come. Give your whole life to Jesus in order to make Him known to the people of Nepal."*

Auntie sat down. Then Birendra stood, **blind but willing to go to Nepal.** Birendra was guided to the front of the church. The crowd listened with hushed attention as Birendra sang in a rich baritone, "The

Mansubba, used Laubach literacy charts.

love of God is greater far than tongue or pen can ever tell."

Then Manu stood up. Sunlight streamed through the window on her face. Her testimony was brief and clear.

> *"Jesus said to me, 'Manu, you don't have full knowledge of the Bible, but you do know about salvation and My love for all people. Will you go to Nepal to speak for Me?'*
> *"I said, 'Yes, Lord, your will be done.'"*

I bowed my head and thanked God for the beginning of a new day in Nepali work, a day in which the Nepali Christians themselves were assuming the burden of the missionary task.

God had opened the door to Nepal, and now He was opening the Nepalis' hearts to serve Him, even on "The Great Day."

Christmas in India

Nepali women squatted in front of mud stoves, cooking their evening rice. Flickering light from the wood fires cast long shadows over their faces. It was Christmas Eve, the evening of *Bura Din* ,"The Great Day," as it is called in India.

There was no snow, no crowds of weary shoppers, no decorated shops in the marketplace to remind us of the holiday. But from a distance came a sound in the chill Indian night. The local Nepali Christians, a small but a happy handful, were gathered in procession. They were singing a foreign tune, but the words were clear: "Joy to the world, the Lord is come!" They sang triumphantly. Children tagged along with the carolers.

When it was announced that pictures were to be shown in the market, an interested crowd of onlookers formed. From a kerosene projector a shaft of light illumined pictures of the nativity as the story of the Savior's humble birth was told, convincingly, powerfully.

Later that evening the Nepalis returned to their houses, while we gathered in one of the missionary homes to exchange gifts around a simple evergreen decked with a few ornaments and Christmas cards.

Christmas morning dawned bright and crisp. A shy little neighbor boy walked softly to our front door with a gift of six tangerines wrapped in an old cloth. Later another came with a squash.

The tiny mud-walled schoolhouse, our temporary church, was too small for the festive service. So Christmas day we met in the living room of Gurung Cottage. Young and old came happily wearing a new wool scarf or blouse. We sat cross-legged on woven mats. Shy children, both Nepalis and Americans, staged a repetition of the Christmas story. Then the worship service began, all in Nepali. There was no beautifully robed choir, but the congregation sang enthusiastically. Our leader spoke of Jesus and how thankful we must be that He was willing to be the first missionary to bring us salvation.

After the benediction, we rose, stretched and made ready for the annual congregational love feast. Hands, brown and white, large and small, dipped into the piles of steaming rice on "disposable plates" made from banana leaves, and bowls of spicy curry.

The sun hung low over the Himalayan foothills. It was time to go home. For some believers that meant a three to five mile hike over steep, rocky paths. For others it meant caroling and witnessing to their Hindu neighbors on the way back.

Now a full moon flooded the hills in fluorescent light. I tumbled wearily into bed. In the distance rhythmic drums beat out a Hindu dance. But nearer by, winding his way down the narrow path, a Nepali lad sang, "Hark the herald angels sing!" The Gift of gifts! For all who will receive Him! I closed my eyes and thanked Jesus for letting me experience the true meaning of Christmas, and experience it in India! It had been a "Great Day!"

It would be an even greater day when that little acorn began to grow.

Chapter 4

Small Village, Big Vision

Miniature Beginnings

Nature tells us an amazing story. Great things often have small beginnings. A tiny acorn grows into a mighty oak tree.

The start of Mirik Bible School, later to be called Darjeeling Hills Bible School, had a very small beginning. There were no Bible school buildings, no campus, no dormitories, no faculty housing, no governing board and no text books, nor were there any Bible study aids in Nepali. We had only an outdated translation of the Bible in the language of these precious people.

February 1, 1954, five Nepali students sat around the Gurung Cottage dining room table. They were Martha Manaen, Martha (Mansubba) Rai, Alice Rai, Miriam (Purna Maya) Thapa, and Shilling Mukhia. Roy, the principal and founder, taught lessons in Nepali, along with Fran Swenson.

Classes were held Mondays, Wednesdays and Fridays. Each week there were scheduled ten hours of classes and ten hours of study. These classes focused first on personal faith and discipleship. Roy taught a basic grasp of biblical truth. The classes also provided ways of learning to present the Gospel to people of other religions. Tuesdays and Thursdays the students fanned out into the neighboring communities and tea gardens, sharing the good news of eternal life through Jesus, using large picture rolls and flannelgraph.

Once a month there was a day of prayer. We all prayed for an outpouring of God's Spirit as well as for a plot of land for the Bible school and for better facilities. Our eyes were on the Lord, who hears and answers prayer.

Sunday was market day, when villagers from all the surrounding areas poured into Mirik for the week's shopping. After church in the tiny mission grade school, the students made good use of preaching opportunities in the market. Other days they washed their own clothes and took turns cooking meals.

A vital part of the Bible school program was mutual sharing. We saw that the life of the group and the effectiveness of the ministry was dependent upon a working fellowship.

Missionaries and students alike gathered in a circle of comradeship and prayer to make the needed decisions. Gradually leadership was given over to the Nepalis.

Should there be a change in the school schedule? Should a Nepali house be built to accommodate the men students who would be coming in? Should a quarterly Bible school bulletin be printed? If so, who should be in charge? A student is in financial need, should the group

First graduating class of Darjeeling Hills Bible School: Martha Rai, Shilling Mukhia, Alice Rai (standing), and Miriam Thapa (Kamala's Mother).

join in looking to the Lord for the supply of that need?

One evening a month it was my contribution to provide joyful, hilarious games. The students were exceptional in their ability to mimic the amazing foreigners. We laughed until we wept. Our bonds grew closer and stronger.

The objectives of the Bible school were put down after the managing board of the school was formed, as follows:

To help students become fully grown in Christ and well prepared to serve Him in their churches and in establishing new evangelical churches where the Gospel has not yet reached.

To provide the students with an introductory knowledge of the Bible.

To help give the students a mastery of a few important books of the Old and New Testament.

To teach the essential Bible truths with a view to the students teaching others.

To give practical experience in evangelism and adult literacy education.

To serve the community in village uplift and social welfare work.

To strengthen the life and mission of the Church by training servants of Christ in evangelism, Christian education, stewardship, community service, literature production and distribution.

During the monsoon of that first year, we had three students up from the plains to attend Bible school during their vacation. One of the three, Kanchi Maya, had been a Christian for only two years. Shortly after her baptism, someone tried to poison her, but God intervened and spared her life.

Later, when she visited her brother, a Hindu priest, and his family, she was forced into a small room and told she would not be able to leave until she was willing to deny Jesus. She refused to deny her Lord. One day when the whole family gathered beside her door, she took a sharp Nepali knife (*kukri*)[12] down from the wall and, holding it out before her, quietly opened the door, walked right through the midst of the awe-struck family and fled without harm.

Just a few days before leaving Bible school to return to the hot plains, Kanchi Maya came for a chat. "Older sister, will you please

―――――――――――――――
[12] Kukri: commonly-used, foot-long, curved Nepali knife.

forgive me for the trouble of heart I gave you when I first came to Mirik. When I came, my cup was dry and empty. I wanted to leave, but God prevented me. The lessons I have learned in Bible school have become very sweet, and now my cup is full and running over. I'm eager to get back to witness to many hundreds of patients who come to the hospital."

We sent her back with many blessings. She was only one of many who would leave refreshed and trained for future fruitful service.

An acorn had sprouted and an oak tree was growing in Mirik. History was being made here in Mirik and elsewhere.

Another Door Opened

The door to Nepal was truly opening. The Catholics from India, led by Father M. Moran, had been traveling to Nepal since 1949 to begin an educational program in Kathmandu. Pat and Hilda and their team were the first to pioneer Protestant medical work in Nepal.

Dr. Bob Fleming, an ornithologist teaching at Woodstock School in hilly Mussoorie, north of Delhi, had been invited by aristocratic students from hermit Nepal to study the exotic birds of their country. Dr. Bob would later document his findings.[13] When Dr. Bob took a medical doctor along into Nepal on his bird hunting trips, the party soon realized the staggering medical needs there. Dr. Bob's wife, Dr. Bethel, was also a medical doctor.

A letter from K.A. Dikshit, Assistant Secretary, Department of Foreign Affairs, Kathmandu, dated May 18, 1953, gave permission for the Flemings and Friederickses to set up a hospital in Tansen and clinics in Kathmandu valley.[14]

It was an unforgettable day when the Flemings, both Dr. Bob and Dr. Bethel, arrived in Kathmandu in October 1953 to begin the first Protestant medical work in Kathmandu valley.[15]

---

[13] Robert L Fleming, Sr., Robert L Fleming, Jr. & Lain Singh Bangdel, *Birds of Nepal: With Reference to Kashmir and Sikkim*, Nature Himalayas; 3rd ed edition 1984.

[14] Lindell, Jonathan, *Nepal and the Gospel of God*, United Mission to Nepal, 1979.

[15]Fletcher, Grace Nies, *The Fabulous Flemings of Kathmandu: the story of two doctors in Nepal*, E.P. Dutton & Co. 1964.

Then Nepal's Door Opened

Responding to the government's invitation, eight Protestant missions then collectively formed, on March 9, 1954, the United Christian Mission, later renamed The United Mission to Nepal (UMN). By 1978, twenty-eight mission organizations from many nations were working together as members of UMN.

Kathmandu was the capital of Nepal, a hotdog-shaped country 120 miles by 500 miles, tucked in between China and India. Along the northern border rose the high Himalaya mountains, most majestic in all the world, cold and impenetrable. The southern border was stifling hot like India.

Nepali legend says that Kathmandu valley was originally a beautiful lake but that a demon god struck the hill that retained the water, thus releasing the water through a gorge, leaving a fertile valley. Perhaps it was an earthquake in years gone by.

At any rate, the valley was productive and full of some two thousand holy spots, all within 204 square miles. Garishly painted gods and goddesses decorated the countless temples. Oxen could not be used within one mile of Hindu temples, so cultivating was mostly done by hand.

Becky Grimsrud was apparently the only missionary nurse outside of Nepal who spoke Nepali. Now she had been invited to work inside Nepal. Should we close down the dispensary in Mirik and send her off? Hadn't our goal been to minister the life of Jesus inside Nepal? Letting her go seemed like a great loss to the community. Our aim was to have nationals in leadership in Nepal as well as India, so we as a mission felt we should send Becky off with our blessing.

Just after Becky left to work in the Kathmandu Cholera Hospital, opened in February 1954, a Nepali lady, a graduate of a Bible school on the plains, told us that God was leading her to our fellowship. She would be a big help in the literacy training program and Bible teaching. Her name was Rebecca Rai. We gave up one Rebecca and received back another.

Then a request came from Nepal for Fran Swenson to join Becky. Before we had really decided to take this step, news came that the Nepal Government had already granted Fran's permission to enter Nepal. We had prayed for years for such a thing. To refuse the permit would be ridiculous, but to accept it and send Fran meant the crippling of the present Bible school program and losing an efficient Bible-school teacher and literacy helper. Now opportunities were coming so fast we had to make major decisions of faith, and to say "Yes, Lord!" even though we didn't know the future.

The way of faith was to obey God and trust Him to replace workers. God did that. One week after Fran packed her things and left Mirik, a letter came from Subit Tshering, the first seminary-trained Nepali, saying God definitely led him to accept a teaching position at the Bible school. Subit was a fine young man, a gifted preacher, experienced soul winner, and a leader of young people. God had again supplied our need!

Then Roy was faced with an enormous challenge. He was asked to be on a committee to draft a doctrinal statement for UMN. Three others were invited to work with him: Anglican Bishop Robinson, a leader in the United Church of North India; Ralla Ram, the Director of the Regions Beyond Missionary Union; and Mr. Ernest Oliver of Brethren background. Where else in the world did missions of so many different denominations and nationalities all work together under one umbrella? How would these four men work out a statement that included basic beliefs of Methodists, Presbyterians, Baptists and Lutherans? It was a first in mission history. It would take much prayer

Bible School matron, Harka Maya Mukhia (left), Subit Tshering, and Rebecca Rai taught at Darjeeling Hills Bible School for many years. Photograph circa 1956.

and careful thought to have unity in such diversity.

God did answer this prayer. Over the next fifty years the United Mission to Nepal (UMN), of which WMPL was a charter member, would open hospitals, schools, hydroelectric plants, and educate many Nepalis in better health, agriculture and business practices. It would impact the lives of thousands of Nepalis for the better.

Pat and Hilda were instrumental in founding the International Nepal Fellowship (INF). INF began a hospital, a leprosarium and many clinics in and around Pokhara. But neither the foreign personnel of UMN or INF could proselytize or start churches. Both agencies agreed with the government policy that missionaries were free to worship with local believers, but not proselytize. If they were found proselytizing, they could be deported. However, missionaries could work with and encourage the indigenous Nepali church. This turned out to be a unique way of doing mission work. The historic precedent had been missionaries starting and running churches, which often led to problems of dependency. In Nepal, however, the church was begun and led by Christian Nepalis from many places. The church was self-supporting, self-propagating and self-governing from the very beginning.

Before all this came to pass, Roy was appointed by UMN to head up an Adult Literacy Program for Nepal. What a task, what an opportunity! When would Nepal's eyes be open to the value of literacy?

Back Turned, Eyes Shut

Kamal's wife lay in resolute silence in the corner of the porch, her back turned, her eyes shut tight. Nearby on the same floor sat her husband and other Nepalis. They huddled around a tiny kerosene lamp, intent on the books in their hands. A whole new world was opening up to them. They were learning to read from carefully prepared, illustrated and tested primers.

Where did the primers come from?

Because Roy had been put in charge of the UMN Adult Literacy program in a country that was only two percent literate, we had to start from scratch. Dr. Laubach had prepared the basic literacy charts, but there was much more to be done.

"Come to Mirik for Adult Literacy Teacher Training!" we advertised all over Darjeeling District. Four gifted Nepali Christians responded.

They made basic word lists of the five hundred most commonly used Nepali words. They surveyed illiterate villagers like Kamal's wife to learn what subjects they were most interested in. Soon they crafted simple sentences with a carefully progressing vocabulary.

He cut.
He cut wood.
He cut this wood.
He cut this wood with a kukri.
He cuts this wood with a kukri.
He will cut this wood with a kukri.

Then basic Nepali booklets were made, gradually increasing in difficulty. They covered topics such as building latrines, warding off disease, family planning, and nutritional foods to eat. The first basic set of readers was *The Story of Jesus*, and there were books about the God of love who gave His Son for the world. But Kamal's wife would have none of this reading stuff. She pulled a light shawl over her head and stubbornly turned her back.

Kamal, her husband, had been discharged from overseas Gurkha military service the year before. He had become a real believer in Jesus Christ while he was in Malaysia. He had met fine Christians there and had grown in the Lord.

Now he had come home to the wife he had married years before when they were both very young. But they had lived poles apart in separate worlds for many years.

Kamal's voice almost broke as he prayed for his wife that her proud stubbornness would be broken, that she would be open to the things of God and to reading. Day by day the literacy teacher sat patiently by Kamal's wife, gently encouraging her, loving her. After five days of flat refusal, Kamal's wife sat up and very shyly glanced at the book. Softly she repeated the words. Soon she was reading phrases.

Kamal's wife was symbolic of the country of Nepal, proud but shy, fearful of the unknown. For many years Nepal had turned her back and shut her eyes to literacy and the things of the living God. It had been in a deep sleep. But no longer. A new day was dawning. Nepal was learning that a whole different world opens when one can read. But what would Nepal read? That was a crucial matter!

We would need to supply an unusual kind of missionary.

The Flat Missionary

Nepal needed a missionary that would never need cholera shots, never get amoebic dysentery, could speak the language like a national, had a simple budget, and didn't worry about being carried across shaky rope bridges high over rushing mountain streams. Nepal needed the "flat missionary".

That flat missionary was a tract, booklet, magazine or book. But to get that missionary to its destination more was needed than a call from God, shopping lists and farewell parties. Much prayer and much work were required.

We had to train Nepali nationals to write for their own people. The writers could not use big pompous words. They had to use simple words from a basic word list. They would write for those who had never heard of Jesus. They needed to describe a God who was the true, living God, not one of the thirty-million Hindu gods. When they wrote of sin, they had to explain that it was not killing a fly but rather grieving God's heart of love. When they wrote of Jesus' sacrifice, they had to show that Jesus did not kill a goat and believe the blood shed would grant favor with the gods. Instead the blood shed was Jesus' own, and He was the Son of the Living God.

After the first original writings, we mimeographed tracts, lesson materials, and even a small illustrated *Luther's Catechism*.

Before long, the Bible school students stood peering curiously into the heavy wooden chest Roy had brought from Kurseong. It contained lead printing type, or "lead soldiers," as Benjamin Franklin had called them.

Would the students help sort the type? Not an easy job, but soon the task was accomplished. Then a carpenter planed boards in our cookhouse to make shelves for printing paper and type. Roy found a simple hand-operated press in Calcutta for ten U.S. dollars. It could only print eight inch wide text and could be carried under one arm. He soon hired Budhiman Rai, a trained printer, to manage the mini press in our cookhouse, and the quality improved.

The winter breezes whistled through the cracks in the wall and made the printing ink very stiff. Even the press was stiff and creaky when the oil in its joints got cold. But Budhiman plodded on. He painstakingly set each letter by hand. Next he smeared ink on the round twelve inch diameter distribution plate. The rollers ran over the plate and then over the type. It took one whole day to compose and print three-hundred copies of one page, but it was a beginning.

Before long Gospel tracts, Bible study guides and even Christmas cards were rolling off that small press. Then *Sangati*, meaning Fellowship, was prepared. It was the first Christian magazine in Nepali. The first four Darjeeling Hills Bible School (DHBS) graduates wrote the entire *Sangati*: Martha, Alice, Shilling, and Miriam Thapa. Then we sent it to as many Nepali Christian groups as we could find.

There still wasn't a single lesson in Nepali for Sunday school teachers. So we busily translated, illustrated, corrected and then finally printed some Nepali Sunday school lessons.

By the time the first class of Bible school students graduated, we

Budhiman Rai using the first mini-press to print "flat missionaries".

had four Nepali missionaries trained and a number of flat missionaries ready to be carried across Nepal's shaky rope bridges.

Just as a flat missionary had made its way into Kathmandu, where Pooba Manab was imprisoned, missions worldwide had learned that Christian literature was a critical component in their programs. So too in our work, many more flat missionaries needed to be prepared with prayerful care. We had been entrusted with the knowledge of the living God. We had been admonished by Him to pass the message of life, of hope, and of an eternal Gospel in Jesus Christ on to trustworthy Nepalis.

They were to follow the Lord's teaching and His compassionate purpose to establish His church, not only in Nepal, but wherever Nepalis were to be found. That meant that not only their lives but the publications coming forth would nurture, train, and establish new believers in the glorious Gospel of Jesus. We needed to reach those who could read but also those who would become new readers.

How could this be done? First, by seeking the Lord's mind and heart in prayer. Jesus was the center, the hub of the Christian literature wheel. The spokes of the wheel went out in writing, editing, artwork and printing. Then there would be departments for advertising, bookkeeping, mail orders, selling, colporteurs, bookmobiles, libraries, and bookshops. The literacy program would also distribute vital literature.

What would the new literates buy? What would they want and need? What message would get their attention and grip them? Roy was challenged to learn all he could about the furtherance of the Gospel by the printed page. Now that Nepal had opened its door for medical and educational workers, and now that there were trained Christian Nepalis coming forth to work there, the demand was all the greater for good flat missionaries. They would not come forth easily.

Tried and Tested

But while we considered these things, life in the village was not without tests. Our Karl Stephen was born in 1955. He was a good baby, so easy to care for. But that year, five-year-old Paul was in bed for three months with a lung infection. We continued to declare the healing power of Jesus over those little lungs.

The manuscripts for the basic literacy primers, *The Story of Jesus*, waited at the printers in Bombay for eight months with nothing done. Finally we had them sent back. We then printed them at a less sophisticated press in Darjeeling. Tests!

Our milk often soured overnight. The meat bought on Sunday, the only day it was available, had to be canned to last the week.

We were driving to Darjeeling with a very sick year-old Kenny to see the doctor. But to my surprise Roy hitched the trailer up to the jeep for the trip. In Darjeeling Roy announced, "Happy Birthday, Honey. Mrs. Winward is selling her kerosene refrigerator." What a gift!

The fridge was loaded into the trailer. Half way back to Mirik we heard a loud crack! Rumble, rumble. We found the trailer hitch, a four-inch square beam, had snapped off. The trailer and fridge lay upside down behind us on the road. Fortunately the trailer had not rolled on down the mountainside.

Just then the Darjeeling Civil Surgeon and his husky driver drove up. They stopped to help us load the fridge into the back seat of the jeep. Then we were off again, with four adults and three children crammed into the front seat and around the fridge.

Heavy fog set in as well as the dark. We crept along at a snail's pace. We arrived in Mirik an hour later, full of praise for God's protection and mercies. I wondered how many angels traveled with us that day.

I was amazed that the fridge worked beautifully, even after such a shake-up. Tests!

We needed to order firewood from a forest depot below Mirik. Our new missionary, Herman Simrose, climbed into the jeep with Jonathan Thapa, Roy, David and Paul. Roy drove through the level area of tall pine trees just outside Mirik. As he crested the ridge, the jeep gained speed. Approaching the first steep, sharp hairpin curve, he stepped on the brakes to shift into low gear—but the pedal hit the floor. There were no brakes! If he turned to the right and into the hill, he thought the jeep would roll over. So he tried to make the curve.

The jeep made it partly around the curve but then flew off the embankment to land thirty feet below against a small tree only five inches in diameter. Herman, Jonathan, and David were all thrown out, landing in a rocky ravine beyond the jeep. Paul and Roy stayed in the jeep.

Had the little tree not stopped the jeep, the vehicle would have rolled down over those who had fallen out. Miraculously everyone walked away from the accident. Our praise to the Lord was profuse for days. Friends helped lower the jeep from "the American shortcut" to the next level of the road. It was towed back to Gurung Cottage, where Clarence stripped it to check for cracks and damage and then put it all back together again.

Months later Roy felt very weak. The Darjeeling doctors sent him to a Calcutta hospital. The diagnosis was a damaged heart muscle from vitamin deficiency at high altitudes. After a month's rest and masses of Vitamin B injections he was much improved and ready to join the family. He missed the first graduation of the Bible school.

We were learning that when we are being tested it is our opportunity to allow Him to change us. "Nought but in love permitted." [16] "You tested us and refined us like silver." Zechariah 3:9 Tests!

Herman Simrose and Betty Hansen walked down the flower-bedecked path to Gurung Cottage to take their marriage vows. We were given permission to rent the land around Clarence's house. Herman began an experimental farm, all with government approval. The farm opened many opportunities for sharing the best seed of all, God's Word. Herman dug a well and installed a hand pump, which supplied water to the Bible school as well as sixteen homes nearby.

By mid December our family was bound for a rest on the warm plains of India. After a refreshing time in the sunshine, we went to the railway station in Calcutta, ready to buy our tickets back to the hills, when we suddenly found out that trains were no longer going to our part of Bengal. Political disturbances had canceled all trains.

But Bible school was about to begin and we had to return. The only alternative was to fly. However, almost all our money was in our bank account in Darjeeling. It was very difficult to cash out-of-town checks in India. We made air reservations in faith. That afternoon a money order from the States came to us in Calcutta, forwarded from Mirik. Father God wanted us back in Mirik. He was faithful, through all the tests. He would even provide jolly Tibetans to help us.

---

[16] Amy Carmichael, *Gold by Moonlight*, London: SPCK, 1935, 6th ed., p. 95, 1943.

Tibetan Car Jacks

Yes, God was faithful even when six-year-old David was troubled with tonsillitis. Dr. Meg Patterson prescribed taking out the tonsils. It took five hours for us to drive fifty miles by jeep along the main trade route to Tibet before we reached Kalimpong.

Dr. Meg performed the tonsillectomy at the Scots Mission Hospital. The hospital was so busy that there was not a single bed available for David, so we arranged for him to stay at the Graham Homes Hospital three miles away.

Roy carried a very sedated David into the jeep and had just begun the drive to the "Homes" when we heard a loud "Psst!" In a minute one of the jeep's tires was flat. Then we found that our tire jack was still at the garage where the jeep had just been repaired.

While Roy got out the spare tire, some jolly Tibetan men swaggered by. With a lot of hand motions we asked the whole group to help us. With a great heave and not a few grunts, they lifted up the jeep as Roy quickly shoved a box under the axle. He changed the tire, and then the men raised the jeep until Roy could pull out the box and then lowered it back down. We were once again ready to drive.

We thanked the men with one word in Tibetan: *"Tu-che-chay."*

Then we thanked the Lord even more for His faithful provision of those friendly "Tibetan car jacks."

David was none the worse for his "uplifting" trip. But we were getting ready for an important, refreshing trip.

Chapter 5

On the Move

Refreshing

When we first arrived in India with intentions of ministering to Nepal, Nepal was still closed to the Gospel. We didn't know the language. There was no Bible school in the language of the Nepalis to train national witnesses. There were no literacy charts to teach illiterate Nepalis how to read their own language.

Five years had gone by. We had endured tests of every sort. Now it was time for furlough. We packed basic essentials into the big blue steel drums again, safe from moisture, bugs and rats. Everything else was then disposed of prior to leaving for the States.

Now Nepal's door had opened to Christians. We had a good start in learning the language. A Bible school had been set up for Nepalis. We had two Nepali teachers in the school and an advisory board of fourteen nationals and two missionaries. Seven acres of land had been bought for the school. A Christian printing press had been established, and the language had been put into literacy charts by Dr. Laubach. All this was in answer to prayer. Folk all around the world had been praying for Nepal and for us.

There was so much to praise God for. In order to return to India, we needed "No Objection to Return" permits from the government. These permits had been granted, and miraculously, tickets to the States for all six of us were in hand. God had wonderfully answered prayer. The Bergs would take the responsibility of the Bible school. It was time to go back for sharing and renewal.

It didn't take long to reach the warm plains and board a Delhi-bound train. The boys, now seven, five, three, and one, were bursting with excitement.

As black, sooty smoke belched out of the steam locomotive, it came pouring into the open windows of our second-class compartment. The boys clung to the window bars, taking-in the new sights and sounds. Wooden-wheeled oxcarts, drawn by water buffaloes, creaked on roads parallel with the railway tracks. Over the plains hung a cloud of fine yellow dust billowing skyward from anything that moved. Our clothes, hands and faces all got dirtier by the minute.

When the train shuddered to a stop at stations, bedlam broke loose. Would-be passengers clamored to get into the compartment while the arriving passengers shoved valiantly to get out.

"*Garam cha. Garam cha.*" Dozens of poorly-clad vendors walked up and down the platform hawking their wares of hot sweet tea, bananas and tangerines, or spicy tarts. Our boys soon learned they could have fruit that they themselves peeled.

Pitiful beggars, wrapped in clotted rags, shoved a tin cup at us pleading for coins.

The needy humanity of India was heart wrenching. Everywhere we looked we saw souls, souls, souls whom Jesus loved and for whom He died.

After a day and a night on the grimy train we pulled into Delhi, all needing a scrub from top to toe. Everything worn in the train needed laundering. I washed clothes by hand while Roy and the boys explored nearby streets.

Hagen family, back in America in 1957. Alma, Karl and Roy in back, Paul, Ken and David in front.

It was raining. The newly washed clothes hung limp. The next day we were to fly to Kabul, Afghanistan. We packed the still-damp clothes in our suitcases and took off.

Dazzling sunshine, crisp air, and a cloudless blue sky welcomed us to Kabul. Our kind German hosts gave us cheerful permission to empty our suitcases to dry in the spacious patio. How I praised God for His sunshine!

After leaving Afghanistan we relished the warmth and love of Momsey's cousins in Germany. My long-unused childhood German was hilariously mixed up with Nepali as I tried to chat with cousins who didn't speak English. Big soft feather beds were a delight to weary little boys. Then came snowballs and snow forts.

We flew Lufthansa to New York. The airline hostess graciously took orders, asking the boys if they would like ham or turkey.

"Turkey, and could I please have the feathers!" declared our Kenny. We had some explaining to do!

The only chicken Ken had seen prepared in India always arrived alive at the door. The boys saved the tail feathers to poke into a big cork which became a great toy. Our boys played with Nepali children and see who could kick the cork, keeping it in the air the longest.

For the folks back home, we would also have some explaining to do about the desperate needs of India.

To the Valleys

We spent our first furlough at the Minneapolis WMPL Mission Headquarters. Momsey left college teaching at 75 to join us. She read countless books to our little men.

Before we returned to India, the directors of the Minneapolis Ebenezer Home graciously arranged for Momsey to live there. We were so thankful for God's provision for her.

As we left for India, we prayed that the Holy Spirit would enable us to speak the Word, to print the Word, and to live the Word. Our hearts were full of joy because Jesus had come to redeem us and to live in our hearts. He had called us to go back to India, and had promised to be with us. Already he had transformed mountains of impossibilities and hills of difficulties into a place of singing. Now it was time for us to go back to "valleys" to reach lost Nepalis for Him.

"Down from the summit, where high inspiration
Fired our souls with a vision of truth,
Down to the valley where hearts are the sorest,
Groping for one to comfort and soothe.

"Down let us go with the fragrance of heaven,
Down, without halting, in Christ-given strength.
Then He can labor through us, as His channels,
He'll be the glorious victor at length!"

Frieda Martini Buchen

Back in India, our family moved to a larger two-story wooden house right on the main road between the hospital and Mirik High School. In a reading room in the front of the house, news magazines, literacy materials, tracts and scripture portions were enthusiastically received. Shilling was in charge of the venture and found many opportunities to share his faith and new life in Jesus. He taught literacy classes as well.

As soon as folk learned to read they were given a graded series of *The Story of Jesus*.

Shilling proposed to Mansubba (Martha), but she felt her call to Nepal held priority in her life. She soon left for Kathmandu as a literacy worker. God had great things in store for her there.

Through the Bible school and the literature program, our objective continued to be the laying of a foundation for a national church in Nepal.

Clarence and Helen Hjelmervik returned to the States. Herman and Betty Simrose moved to Amp Pipal, Nepal. Luther and Berit Erickson came to help with the agricultural program in Mirik. Darjeeling-based Monrad Ulvesetter, with Nepal-WMPL, returned to Norway. Monrad's Norwegian co-workers in Nepal worked faithfully alongside our Bible School graduates. They encouraged and supported our vision and goal to enlarge the Bible school and train still more Nepalis.

A New Dedication

The hilltop was alive with activity. Carpenters were busy putting finishing touches on the newly-built classroom. Bible school students were cleaning windows, weeding flowerbeds, and getting their rooms in apple-pie order. The Bible school advisory board's biannual meeting and dedication of this new building were to take place that weekend. It was 1958.

The setting sun cast kindly rays of golden light on the Himalayan foothills. The Mirik mail land rover coming from Darjeeling caught the sunlight and for a moment flashed it back from the windshield. Then it dipped down behind the trees and slowly came to a halt in front of our home. It was loaded with passengers coated with dust.

The out-of-town board members had arrived. Some were pastors and teachers, others were businessmen and church elders. They crawled stiffly out of the land rover and paid their fare.

The next day dawned bright with a sense of expectancy.

The DHBS Advisory Board, 1959, when the new facility was dedicated.

From the time it was first begun, the Darjeeling Hills Bible School had shifted around from one rented quarter to another. Now at long last it was settled. The school was on its own land, just two days before it had moved into the newly finished school building.

The board members left the main auto road and slowly trudged up the newly built Bible school road. They paused to look across the valley into the hills of Nepal about fifteen miles westward, and then to the towering Himalayas in the north. Between them and the "snows" lay steep hills and valleys dotted with mud homes. The men pressed on to the top of the hill to see the new building. From its doors young men and women would go forth prepared to bring the good news of salvation to Nepalis far and near.

The board, composed of thirteen nationals and three "Europeans," gathered for their meeting in the light, airy classroom. They reviewed in brief the activities of the past year. A men's hostel eighteen feet by twenty-six feet, a school building, a water pump and two toilets with septic tanks had been completed. All this was done without incurring any debt or making direct solicitations for funds. Ten former students were serving the Lord full time.

As the crimson sunset cast a warm glow over our home, we sat eating curry and rice. We thought of the highlights of the meeting. Mahendra, principal of a high school in Darjeeling, said, "You know, I had been trying to think of a scheme for earning money for the Bible school. After hearing the report of how the Lord has supplied all the needs this past year, I have seen that prayer is the best way!"

The sunset light changed to yellow-gold and finally into pearl. Our hearts were full of praise to our King and Shepherd who had so wonderfully supplied. We had witnessed but a beginning of God's work which we believed would continue. The approaching darkness reminded us of the urgent words of Jesus,

"As long as it is day, we must do the work.
Night is coming, when no man can work."[17]

The following day, the local congregation, those who had helped with the building of the school, and others gathered for a church service in the school building as it was dedicated to this one purpose.

Soon son David would attend a school bearing a godly purpose.

---

[17] John 9:4

Back to Darjeeling

It was a big day when we drove seven-year-old David to Darjeeling to enroll in Mt. Hermon School. Mt. Hermon was mainly staffed by New Zealand and Australian teachers, as well as a few Indian teachers. Students came from all over Asia. Students from thirty-two language groups enrolled for this truly cross-cultural education.

Decked out in grey wool trousers, a white shirt and a navy blue blazer, David waved us a brave "Goodbye." We were not permitted to visit him for several months but we could write letters.

David thrived on the excellent teaching and spiritual program at Mt. Hermon, but the boarding arrangements left much to be desired. Ultimately, we decided that the other boys and I should move to Darjeeling. We would move to the Scots Mission House #2. In true British fashion, homes in Darjeeling were generally known by name rather than house number.

The Scots Mission House was a large round building divided into three sections. It was sandwiched in between Turnbull Boys School and the Nepali Girls Boarding School. It had been the home of missionaries for many years. David would live at home and attend school as a "day scholar" (or "day scowler" as Paul suggested.) Dan Mit, who had helped us when we first arrived in India, would come back to us and assist us in the kitchen. Roy would stay on in Mirik and come to Darjeeling on weekends.

I found leaving Mirik more difficult than leaving America. We had become part of a warm community. Our neighbors begged me not to leave. But familiar words came to my mind:

"If place I seek or place I shun,
      the soul finds happiness in none;
But with my God to guide the way,
      'tis equal joy to go or stay."

God's commands are His enablings, so the children and I packed up. Roy was released to give full time to Christian Nepali literature and Bible translation. We lived in one side of the Scotts Mission House adjacent to the cookhouse. The Scottish Presbyterian family, Jim and Beth Brodie, lived in the other half. The Brodies and we would cook in our indoor kitchens, leaving the cookhouse vacant.

When Roy moved back to Darjeeling, the mini Mirik press had to be moved too. The many trays of heavy lead type were carefully wrapped in separate packages and hauled to Darjeeling. Roy searched high and low for a suitable spot to work in, but none was to be found. So the mini press went back to a cookhouse, the Mission House cookhouse. But this time there were cement walls and flooring instead of wooden walls and a mud floor.

The Mirik Press was now transformed into JJP Press, *Jiwan Jyoti Prakashan*, or Light of Life Publishing. But in cold Darjeeling the ink got hard and sometimes uneven. It was time to find a better machine.

For months, mission friends and we prayed for a larger, more efficient press. Finding the rapidly growing work quickly outstripped the capacity of the local printers, Roy took a bold step and bought an Indian-made treadle press for six hundred dollars, more than two year's salary for the average person in India.

It was a momentous day when our new press arrived. A large truck drove into the Mission compound and backed right up to the cookhouse verandah. Sixteen available Tibetan and Nepali porters were called in. It took them four hours to gradually lever the two large crates, each one weighing half a ton, from the truck to the cookhouse. At last we had a press that would allow us to do what God assigned us to do. With very little overhead to speak of, we recovered the initial capital investment within two years.

The new press "officially" operated by electricity. However, local power demand was far greater than the capacity of the Darjeeling generating system. Streetlights often glowed a dim orange, just sufficient to see the top half of the pole. The way-overloaded electrical system sometimes dragged the power from a nominal 220 volts down to 93 volts. This was not enough to run the press. So the printing team went on "night duty" when fewer people used electricity. "Kalink kalank," we could hear the faithful work of Budhiman and his men working far into the night.

The work grew phenomenally. Every available inch of the three little rooms of the cookhouse, including the verandah, was used for type racks, paper storage, printing and bookbinding. Our Mission House #2 had a large closed-in porch. This became the accounting and dispatch office. In one month 130,000 tracts were printed.

The Nepali literature snowball had started rolling which no one would stop. We scrambled to get more manuscripts and better distribution outlets.

Eventually the World Mission Prayer League's publishing effort joined hands with the Scots Mission work in 1960 to form the NISS, *Nepali Isai Sahitya Sangha*, (The Nepali Christian Literature Society). The United Mission to Nepal (UMN) and the Eastern Himalayan Church Council (EHCC) were also charter members.

Dinesh Khaling, a Nepali college graduate, went on to get his diploma in journalism at Hislop College. Valued writers, like Adon Rongong and Solon Karthak, contributed greatly toward good manuscripts. In 1962, Dorthy Barker from Australia came to help with artwork. Their efforts would all be a tremendous blessing to Nepal.

We were now a publishing house - but without a house. We prayed we would soon be able to move out of the cookhouse and our verandah into a building suited for preparing, printing, storing and selling literature. We continually felt the urgency of the times, and our need to be useable at all costs, and pliable to His will in all things. We wrote "The responsibility is so great, the calling so high, the honor so tremendous that we need an army of praying ones to keep us true and keen for the Lord."

There was another who would be invited to be useable and pliable to God's will.

On One Lung and Prayer

The invitation sent to Shilling was like no other. After some seventy visits to government offices over a period of nine months, Jonathan Lindell finally received permission to work in the hilly areas of Nepal, outside the Kathmandu valley. The UMN invited Shilling to join Jonathan, Ron Byatt and Hem Lal to begin a community service project in the Gorkha area. That meant going beyond the Kathmandu valley, out into a world vastly different from Darjeeling or Kathmandu. Darjeeling houses were built of wood and Kathmandu houses made of clay bricks, but the Nepal mountain people built their homes of stone and mud, or bamboo and mud. They farmed differently, and even their dialects were different.

Shilling agreed to join the team. It was February, 1957. Even with only one lung he was willing to go where the Lord directed. It took a week to travel from Kathmandu to Amp Pipal. The men forded six rivers on the way. Seven porters assisted the team of four with their initial equipment.

Amp Pipal lay nestled high on the crest of a hill, overshadowed by the majestic Dhaulagiri mountain range. The team received permission to pitch a tent in the village headman's field. There was no lumber available, nor were there tables, benches or chairs. Everything had to be done on the ground. Cooking was done over an open fire.

Hundreds of enthralled villagers watched every movement of this unusual team. Many had never seen white skin before. The men helped the locals understand why they had come. Unrolling a chalkboard, the men showed a picture of a school, a house with medical help, fields with a barn, and a Bible. They explained that these men were all Christians. They followed the instructions in that book and had come to help the community. The local officials welcomed them. Jonathan would later document the growth of the Gospel in Nepal.[18]

The government gave permission to cut down some trees to make boards and eventually tables and chairs. The only local tools were axes (for shaping doors and window frames) and stone hammers (for shaping stones for houses). Gradually, a school building was constructed. Then classes, held at first under the trees, moved inside.

Step by step, a simple dispensary was built. Our own Becky Grimsrud from Mirik and Nora Vickers came to work there. But their medical cases were anything but simple. Gunshot wounds, serious burns, TB, and bear-maul wounds were often the order of the day.

After four years of ministering in Nepal with Darjeeling Hills Bible School graduates, Becky wrote to us, "More than ever I feel that the Bible school is the best contribution missionaries can make working together with Nepali colleagues."[19]

Martha Mansubba Rai had studied hard in Kathmandu to complete her high school work. She received an award from Nepal's queen for having the highest high school finishing score in all of Nepal. Later she and Unamani Pradhan joined the Amp Pipal team as literacy workers. Unamani had also studied in Darjeeling Hills Bible School.

Gradually a house was built of local stone for Jonathan and Evie and their four daughters. The next year, when our family hiked up to

---

[18] Lindell, Jonathan, *Nepal and the Gospel of God*, United Mission to Nepal, 1979.

[19] Becky Grimsrud, private correspondence to Roy and Alma Hagen, 1958.

Amp Pipal to visit the Lindells, we were the first foreign family to visit them. When the local Nepalis learned we had four sons, a sign of great favor among Hindus, they asked, "What kind of a caste are these Christians? If they have daughters, they have only daughters. If they have sons, they have only sons!"

Before long, Shilling proposed to Martha again. This time she felt it was right to accept. Becky, Shilling and Martha all came back to Darjeeling for the wedding. Our friends in the Nepali church prepared five hundred banana-leaf plates and a wedding feast of curries and deep-fried pastries.

A kindly October sun shone down on Darjeeling the day of their wedding. Christians and Hindus alike gathered from far and near for the occasion. Martha's brother, who had forbidden her ever to return home if she became a Christian, attended the wedding. The strains of *I'd Rather Have Jesus than Silver or Gold* filled the church as the two knelt before the altar. Shilling and Martha were both faithful in giving praise to God alone for all He had done in their lives.

They returned to Amp Pipal where vegetables and meat were scarce, where villagers had no soap but soaked clothes in wet ashes, where thousands had never heard the name of Christ.

Shilling became principal of the school, a spiritual shepherd of the few Christian believers, and a friend and counselor of many.

They kept in touch with us so we would know how to intercede for them. When they had been there five years, Shilling wrote:

"In our project area a lot of changes have taken place. All the team members are busy with our daily duties. We are planning to open a high school in a nearby village as well as build a fifteen-bed hospital. I am supervising building work, the boys' hostel and the school work. Moreover, I have a lot of opportunity to present Christ to the people here. In the morning before school starts, I take the attendance of the workmen and then present the Gospel for some time to them. Three of the leading leaders have admitted the Deity of Christ. Please remember them in your daily prayer. We are not allowed to preach as yet. Don't know how long it will be like this. But the Almighty God knows all about it and for sure He will open a door to reach the Gospel to these folk."

Shilling lived out the principle of cooperation without competition in Nepal, even though it could sometimes be hilarious!

Chapter 6

Nothing Monotonous

The Comedy of Comity

Cooperation without competition is an important concept in mission circles. The official word for such an agreement is comity, but it turned into comedy one Sunday after our Lutheran mission agreed to work in comity with the Scottish Presbyterians. They had been in the Darjeeling District for eighty years. Under the comity understanding we respected their work, and we were free to learn the language, teach, preach, and train workers for future work in Nepal. But we were not to start another church. We had a mutual agreement that we would not compete with their ministry.

For the benefit of our children, we often attended a Scottish Presbyterian service conducted in English. (The boys spoke and understood everyday Nepali conversation but Nepali sermons were generally beyond their ability or attention span.)

When we had a communion service there, it was the custom for aging Pastor "Daddy Duncan" first to serve the two "elders," who would then distribute the elements to the rest of the congregation. He would hand out a piece of bread to one "elder" who would pinch off a tiny piece, and then he would hand another piece to the other "elder" to pinch off a piece. The men would hold the remaining bread until the pastor reached out to take it for serving to the congregation.

But one day "Daddy Duncan" was ill. So his son Jim came from nearby Kalimpong to officiate.

The service began with the usual opening hymns. Two brand-new missionaries, a tall Norwegian and an American WMPLer, were the "elders" that day. The two sat in their unaccustomed but appointed places on the front row. Jim took two quite large pieces of bread, at least a quarter of a slice each. He presented one piece to the American, and the other one to the Norwegian and then focused on reading the Bible passage.

The American dutifully popped the whole piece of bread into his mouth, closed his eyes, bowed his head and prayed. The Norwegian thought to himself, "That's an awful big piece of bread. Wish he would give me some juice to wash it down with." But he, too, ate the whole thing, closed his eyes, and prayed. Both men were indeed thankful for the body of Jesus broken for them and for His blood shed for sinful mankind.

After finishing reading the scriptures, Jim stretched out his hand to receive the bread back again from the American, expecting a tiny bit to have been pinched off, but it was all gone. Completely aghast, he turned to receive the rest of the bread back from the Norwegian, only to find out that he too had eaten the whole thing. It took more than a few seconds for Jim to regain his dignified Scottish composure. Fortunately there was more bread available for the rest of the congregation. And the two new missionaries were learning what "comity" really meant!

We laughed over the "comedy of comity," but we laughed even more over the things our children said.

Out of the Mouth of Babes

God often used our children to remind us to laugh. There were many memorable moments when laughter was the best response at the time, and the retelling has provided much more laughter over the years. Here is a sampling:

Four-year-old Karl and I were walking to the vegetable market. His brothers were all at school. He was kicking a stone soccer-fashion back and forth across the path.

"Hurry up, Karlie! You're my slowpoke!"

"You're my fastpoke!" came his reply.

Our house helper saw Paul digging in the garden. She asked, "What are you doing, Paul?"

"I'm planting meat!" came his confident reply.

Karl jumped down from a tree where he had been climbing. As he landed on the ground, his pants split from belt to belt. He came running into the house calling,

"Mommy, Mommy! Tragic magic!"

The boys had a schoolmate, Nicholas, who had a plaster cast on his broken leg. The boys had great fun signing their names on "Nick's" cast.

Staying in our home at the time we had an eccentric journalist who came to breakfast either smoothing his hair or holding together his button-missing shirt.

Remembering his friend Nicholas, nicknamed "Nick," Kenny innocently asked, "Your name is Dick! Is that short for ridiculous?"

Karl, having just received some hand-me-down clothing, said, "Mommy, can you thin my pants?

We had just arrived in a small Austrian hotel. While I was unpacking, the boys were exploring the hallways. I overhead Kenny shouting, "What does WC stand for?"

From the end of the hall, a helpful brother shouted back, "That means 'Women Coming!'"

Kenny, practicing his trumpet, asked, "How do I play the note with the tic-tac-toe sign?"

Karl wrote to his older brother, summarizing learning to drive, "I'm getting plenty of good driving practice. It is rather difficult though, because I can't reach the clutch or brake and gas and see out the windshield at the same time. It is easier driving backwards because I can see better out the back of the jeep."

It was bedtime in Mission House #2. Kenny was in the bathroom. Karl knocked on the door. "Let me in. I've got to go!"

"This isn't your bathroom!" came the reply from within.

"Then whose is it?" Karl asked.

"It's the Mission's!" answered Ken.

"No it isn't. It's God's!" Karl replied.

Paul, overhearing the conversation, asked, "Isn't everything God's?"

"Yah, but God doesn't need a bathroom! Let me in!"

Jean Raddon had let the Lord into her life, and some of the results included more hilarity.

The Toothless Wonder

Jean Raddon had been one of the pioneering team that began work in Pokhara with Pat and Hilda in 1952. A number of years later, she and a co-worker came to Kalimpong to have a time of rest and relaxation in a lovely guest house called Ahava. The altitude there was lower than Darjeeling, so it was warmer. Jean's bridgework needed repair, so she and her fellow-missionary came to Darjeeling to visit the dentist.

They stopped in to say hello and have a cup of tea, when Jean declared, "We didn't want to 'burden' your busy household, so we decided to book a room near the local market."

"Wherever did you find a room in the bazaar?" I queried. Most decent hotels were further up the hill from the market. Unknowingly, they had booked a room in the Tibetan "red-light-district!"

"Stay for lunch!" I begged them. They graciously accepted my invitation.

During lunch, Jean had four pairs of curious boyish eyes watching her every bite while the boys ate very methodically, never taking their eyes off of her. They wondered how she did it, and just could not figure it out. She was eating lettuce without her teeth!

But that wasn't Jean's last episode with her bridgework, as we learned many years later.

Jean had a Nepali lady, *Didi*, meaning older sister, who helped her with housework. Her thatch-roofed house consisted of bamboo walls and floor fashioned of mud mixed with manure to make it firm. Didi had faithfully boiled the drinking water, pasteurized the milk, shopped in the market, cleaned the rice of stones, washed clothes and did some hundred-and-one things that needed doing while Jean worked in the hospital. Didi had worked faithfully for Jean for twenty-five years.

When time came for Jean to retire, she said to Didi, "You are welcome to anything I have that you would like, pictures, pots and pans, clothes, whatever."

Without hesitation, Didi announced, "Oh, I would like your teeth!"

"But they wouldn't fit you!" Jean replied.

"Oh, but they DO!" came the straightforward answer!

We would laugh about Jean and her bridgework for years to come, but driving our mission jeep during a Communist inspired strike was no laughing matter.

Tailgating the Angels

A once-in-a-lifetime visit with the King, right in the palace! Pastor Stoa of Seattle was describing his personal visit with the King of Norway, as we sat around the dining room table. He soon had another story of a situation that even he could not talk his way through.

He and his wife had come for a quick visit to Darjeeling. Now it was time for us to drive the Stoas down the mountain to Bagdogra, Darjeeling's closest airport. From there they would fly to Calcutta to catch an international flight. Such tickets were not easily changed. They had to make connections.

But then Communist extremists called for a total strike, a "*hartal*," in Darjeeling District. All shops were closed. No vehicles were allowed on the roads, not even bicycles. On previous hartals vehicles that violated the strike had been burned. How were we to get the Stoas safely to the airport?

The Stoas and I committed the whole situation to the Lord. He reminded us that if He opened the eyes of the blind, He could shut the eyes of those who "see." We thanked Him for His protection and started off in our jeep.

We had gone about four miles, as far as Ghoom, when suddenly a police jeep pulled out right in front of us from the Kalimpong road, and continued down the road toward Bagdogra. We tailgated in hot pursuit, speeding on the few straight stretches and slowing down for the many sharp curves. In a number of places, Communist strikers had lowered bamboo barriers across the road, preventing any traffic from passing. But when the strikers saw the police jeep approach, they hurriedly lifted the barrier and let the police and us through.

At one point the police jeep ahead suddenly swung off the main road and took off down the steep Punkabari Road, a shortcut back road to Bagdogra. We followed, whipping back and forth down seven steep hairpin curves. Soon we were cruising through flat tea gardens and before long arrived safely at Bagdogra airport in plenty of time for the Stoas to catch their plane for Calcutta.

I stayed in a Siliguri hotel that evening since the local missionary's guest room was perpetually filled. I thanked God for answered prayer and traveling mercies. There was no hartal the next day. I drove home still rejoicing.

Do angels drive police jeeps? We think they can. They were

driving downhill, but we would soon be required to drive up the mountainside in reverse.

Backwards up to Sandakphu

On the crest of scenic hills and mountains, and in many of the picturesque locations around the world, one can find attractive brown plaques cemented to rocks or posts. These plaques remind viewers of the living God who created all beauty. These plaques are made by the Evangelical Sisters of Mary in Darmstadt, Germany. We had been given one of these praise plaques to mount in a prime location.

Darjeeling was known as the "Queen of the Hill Stations" in India. We were in the "foothills" at 6,500 feet. Morning and evening I would walk out to gaze at the ever-changing view of the Mt. Kanchenjunga range.

Some mornings the mountains were bathed in dazzling sunrise pink. Other days they were totally hidden. The view was seldom the same except after the June to October "monsoon" season, when the mountains stood out in crystal clear splendor day after day against a brilliant blue sky.

Sandakphu was the crown of the hills surrounding Darjeeling. At an elevation of 11,929 feet, it was an ideal spot to view Mt. Everest, the world's highest mountain, as well as Mt. Kanchenjunga, the third highest. Travelers went there to see the sunrise on the peaks before the clouds covered them. It was an ideal spot to put up a praise plaque reminding visitors of our awesome Creator Father God.

Our two youngest sons, Ken and Karl, had a week's school vacation. We had two guests staying with us, and our twenty-fifth wedding anniversary was coming up.

One afternoon Roy suddenly said, "Let's go to Sandakphu!"

For a moment I groaned, wondering how to prepare three meals for six people in about an hour. There were no shops or restaurants on the mountains. But when I realized that we could put up the praise plaque, I stopped moaning. In a short time we got together food, sleeping bags, cement and sand.

We left at four in the afternoon for what we thought would be a five-hour trip up a very narrow steep road. The first fifteen miles we cruised along at 7,000 to 8,000 feet, in and out of beautiful woods. Then the road skirted the Nepal-India border. We showed our passports at a checkpoint, and at five-thirty p.m. we started up thirty-two sharp, steep switchbacks, gaining a foot of altitude every seven feet of road.

We had climbed enough to be looking down on those switchbacks when we heard an ominous sputtering from the engine. The gas wasn't reaching the carburetor. Air was getting into the pump that filtered the gas. We applied soap on the outside of the pump to prevent air from getting in. By frequently hand-pumping the carburetor, we managed to get to the shoulder of the ridge at Tungloo by nine p.m. We were still only one third of the way to Sandakphu. A spiritual battle was on in full force.

Fortunately the travelers' lodge at Tungloo was unoccupied. The watchman in charge gave us permission to spend the night there. We ate tuna sandwiches and crawled into our sleeping bags.

Before Roy went to bed, he made a new gasket out of a paper plate. At two a.m. he was trying to get the jeep going again. At three a.m. the rest of us got up. We sipped Nepali tea and then started.

As long as the jeep was going downhill the engine hummed beautifully. The gas ran into the pump. But then trying to go up the

To keep our ailing jeep running, Roy had to drive in reverse up this last stretch of the steep road to Sandakphu, 11,929 feet altitude.

steep thirty- to forty-degree grade was a different story. The engine stopped countless times.

The fellows pumped the carburetor and we progressed a little further. I had been learning that praising God brings the victory: Satan must flee! He did not want us to put up that praise plaque. I began praising and singing to the Lord that the victory was HIS, that the devil was defeated.

Humanly and mechanically speaking, it was impossible to get up that mountain. But with God all things are possible, and in the name of Jesus we had the victory.

Reaching 10,000 feet, the jeep sputtered to a standstill again. It was a mile and a quarter to reach Sandakphu. Our guests and I got out to lighten the load.

"Let me take the plaque, cement and sand," I begged Roy.

"We'll make it!" he replied.

I kept praising God as we plodded up the steep cobblestone slope. It was six-thirty a.m. when we left the jeep, just as the first rays of sunrise were painting the peaks of Everest. By seven-thirty a.m. the boys and Roy had progressed another 750 feet.

We watched and waited, prayed and praised. Then Roy sent the food and plaque with a passing Nepali who was trudging up to

Because of this view of Kanchenjunga from Sandakphu, it was the perfect place to put the praise plaque.

Sandakphu. I began to cook breakfast on a little wood stove in the lodge.

Meanwhile Roy and the boys turned the jeep around inch by inch by hand. By Roy holding the back and both boys holding the front fenders, they bounced the jeep around to face downhill. Then the gas flowed down into the carburetor.

Still in "low transfer," Roy backed up the last treacherous forty-five-degree slope. There were no guardrails along the hand-built retaining wall. A wrong turn could have sent the jeep hurtling thousands of feet down in the valley below.

My mouth was dry and my knees felt like rubber as we watched from the top. All I could whisper was "Jesus is Victor! Jesus is Victor!"

At last Roy reached the top safely. I felt as though I had fought Satan every inch of the road with the wondrous name of Jesus. Karl helped mix the sand and cement, and before long the plaque was set in place in the center of a huge rock where viewers had full view of Mt. Everest and Mt. Kanchenjunga. The plaque read,

"I will bless the Lord at all times.
His praise shall continually be in my mouth!"
Psalm 34:1

Hallelujah!

We would soon have occasion to bless the Lord, this time with a man-eating leopard on the scene.

A Man-eating Leopard

A man-eating leopard! Better hanging on the wall than out killing villagers!

Ob and Helen Landsverk, who worked among tribal Santals, had invited our family to come away from cold Darjeeling for a visit on the warm plains.

We stood gazing at the enormous leopard skin hanging on their living room wall. Ob explained that particular leopard had killed twenty-six children and adults and countless animals. It would spring at a victim's throat and drag it off.

"Some of the Santals asked me to help kill this one and I shot it!"

Our boys stood in hushed admiration as tall Ob told the story. "The leopard is one of the most dangerous animals in the world. Some African hunters say it is the most dangerous."

"How did you get it?" queried David.

"We tied a goat near the foot of a tree as bait. Some of our Santal men fastened a string bed up in a tree. The bed is called a *machan*.[20] Another fellow and I climbed up the tree. When we heard the goat bleat, my friend shone a flashlight on the leopard and I shot it!"

"Wow!" Paul whispered in awed amazement.

One day while we were at the Landsverks, a tall swarthy Santal gave a slight cough outside their back door. He had come from a village ten miles away.

"Sahib, a leopard has taken four goats in our village. Last night he even dragged off my bullock. Now I have no way to plow. Can you please come and help us, Sahib!"

Ob said he would come. He asked Roy, "Do you want to go along?"

"Sure!" came the swift reply.

The first night they drove off to the village and scouted around for a good tree to hide in. When they found one, Roy climbed up and down the tree hauling guns, pillows and jackets, while Ob went back to the village for the bait, a goat.

By the time Roy got everything up in the tree, it was dark. He realized he had the flashlights and Ob had to carry a goat all the way from the village to the tree in the dark.

"Lord, protect Ob!" he whispered.

Ob had managed to hide the little goat under his jacket. He got to the tree, tied the goat to a stake at the foot of the tree, and then climbed up to wait in hushed suspense. About twenty minutes later they heard the goat get away.

Ob had to climb down, retrieve the goat, and retie it, all the while hoping the hungry leopard wouldn't spring at him from the brush. The wait went on until midnight when they decided to go home. They shone the light around and spotted the leopard more than a hundred yards away, pacing back and forth.

The next afternoon the men went off again. This time they were more calm and assured they would get their animal. The villagers chased cattle and goats ahead of them into the jungle to whet the

---

[20] A wooden framed bed with woven strings as mattress.

appetite of the leopard. Then the villagers called the animals all home again. Ob and one Santal got settled in one tree. Roy and the Santal driver arranged themselves in another tree, about twenty-five feet away. The Santals held the lights ready to shine while Ob and Roy held the guns.

This time two goats were used, one near the tree where Roy waited, the other a little farther off, nearer Ob's tree. Roy had a perfect aim on the nearer goat from where he was squatting but had to stand on the branch to shoot the farther bait.

Again they waited in hushed anticipation in the silence of the dark Indian night.

About an hour later Roy heard the leopard's slow heavy footsteps crunching the leaves directly under his tree. Then they stopped. There was dead silence. The leopard gave a quiet, deep guttural growl. Then there was silence again. Roy squatted with his gun ready. Fifteen minutes later the Santal driver let the water canteen slip and hit against the tree trunk, but there was no other sound. The men sat poised and ready for the next two and a half hours, waiting for the goat's bleating.

Suddenly the farther goat gave a cry of terror, and Roy stood up to take good aim at the leopard. The driver fumbled with the flashlight and couldn't get it on, and Ob's boy couldn't get his on either. The next thing Roy knew, his foot slipped off the branch and he was sprawled on the ground fifteen feet below. Bang! The gun went off as he fell. The other men didn't know who or what was dead, and weren't sure where the leopard was.

Fortunately Roy wasn't even scratched. Getting up as fast as he could, he started to climb the tree. Then he remembered his gun was still lying on the ground.

"Driver, shine the light!" Roy called and found the gun. The driver, normally very brave and patient, was petrified. He later said that he had thought the leopard and Roy were fighting and that the leopard would come up the tree for him next, which was not an impossibility. At the bang of the gun, Ob got his light on the leopard, which was dropping its prey and circling around in Roy's direction – and then ran off. There were sighs of relief and "Thank You" to the Lord when Roy was back up in the tree safe.

The men waited for a long time for the leopard to return for the wounded goat, but it didn't come, so they got down out of their trees and took the goat to the village threshing floor where they tied it up.

They waited unsuccessfully on the top of a haystack hidden by bamboos. Finally at dawn they returned home.

That next night both Ob and Roy had commitments that could not be changed. We were enjoying " *baskiya*," our midmorning tea the following day, when we were interrupted. Ob went to the door to respond to a cough. His voice grew angry and adamant as he spoke with the caller. If only we could have understood Santali.

Finally Ob returned to finish his tea, shaking his head in total amazement. "I can't believe it! That leopard came to the village last night, killed a bullock and gorged himself on it so much that he lay down to sleep right in the village. Instead of calling me to shoot him while he was sound asleep, they cut up the remains of the bullock, cooked it, and had a feast! That half eaten carcass would have been ideal bait to lure the leopard back for us to shoot him!"

"But I've got a surprise for you, Roy," Ob continued. "You'll never guess what the villagers found under the tree you fell out of." Ob handed Roy the keys to Mission House #2, our home in Darjeeling. Those were keys we would soon need, but did not even know were missing.

En route back to Darjeeling, we heard that Ob did kill the leopard. The villagers had made a machan between two nearby palm trees. It hadn't been easy to climb twenty feet up a naked palm and then to crawl out onto a bed which seemed about two feet square. They got double-barrel shotguns and seal-beam-lights all aimed and waited patiently. Every shadow on the ground looked suspiciously like a leopard. Still they waited patiently. Then suddenly they heard the goat bleat. As a Santal shone the light straight at the leopard, Ob had taken careful aim and shot the animal. He shot the leopard a second time just to make sure it was dead.

What shouts of joy were heard all over the village as the Santals heard and realized the dreaded leopard was dead. During this trip to the plains, the Lord had protected us all from the leopard. He had reinforced the truth that we are called to be faithful in our part, even when we do not get to see the exciting ending of the adventures He allows. Another journey would be just as unforgettable and nearly fatal.

Near Fatal Journey

We were on our way to a tiny land only half the size of Connecticut. Sikkim is encircled by Tibet, Bhutan, India and Nepal, a land of magnificent Himalaya mountains, dark forests, green fertile valleys and raging torrents.

With a population (in 1961) of only 130,000 Lepchas, Bhutias and Nepalis, this minute land had worked hard to keep its traditional culture, so much so that, it was one of the few countries in the world that still had no public movie theater.

Forty years of "enlightened rule" was the record of the *Maharajah* of Sikkim, His Highness Sir Tashi Namgyal. Very quiet and slight, he was an ardent Buddhist and renowned artist. These two characteristics were revealed in his writing:

> *"...in this stormy world of strains and tensions, the flower of Sikkim will, beneath the shade of her Protecting Deity of the Snowy Ranges, Kangchenjunga, blossom in sweet and untroubled calm, and that her fragrance will perchance be wafted awhile to other lands, that they may also have joy of it."*

Robi Das, Calcutta's Bible Society Director, and Roy had visited the Maharajah.

An avid painter, the Maharajah had taken them into his studio to display his paintings. His artwork of the Himalayas and of Mt. Kanchenjunga, in particular, had been done in strong, dark colors. Each painting showed large colored bars in the upper left hand corner.

"What do these represent?" Roy asked, inquiring about the bars.

"Those represent the evil spirits ruling over the mountains. You don't believe in evil spirits, do you?" the Maharajah asked.

"Oh yes, we do!" the men replied.

Then Roy queried, "How do you overcome them?"

"I push them back by meditation, but they always return," the Maharaja answered sadly.

Whereupon Roy responded, "In the powerful name of Jesus we can overcome evil spirits and they must leave. When Jesus shed His blood for us, Satan and his demons were defeated." The three men spent the afternoon in an important discussion.

Many Sikkimese believed that Kanchenjunga was a god that ruled over them. Once each year at the Maharajah's palace grounds, there was a celebration called "Worship of the Snowy Ranges." Here colorful pageantry and dances depicted the people's worship.

But not all Sikkimese worshiped the mountains. There were some who had personally come to know the Creator of those mountains and had faith in Him. We were eager to visit the Christians in Gangtok, the capital of Sikkim, and to encourage them in their active program of distributing Nepali Christian literature.

Sparbah Lyngdoh, a friend from Assam and member of the Khasi tribe, came to spend part of his vacation with us in Darjeeling. He had never seen the Himalayas or Sikkim. We felt it was a good time to see Gangtok, visit the members of our Christian Nepali Book and Tract Club there, and witness the annual palace festivities.

The day for our journey dawned grey and misty, but we hadn't driven far on our sixty-five-mile trip to Gangtok before we broke out of the thick clouds. Our road, dappled with light and shade, plunged 5,000 feet down, clinging creeper-like to the mountainside. A few clouds below us in the valley appeared like thin fading puffs of wool. Down, down we wound our way until we reached the muddy raging Tista River, swollen with monsoon rains. Tree trunks floated like match sticks down the river.

After a picnic lunch by the side of the road, we followed the vicious Tista as it carved its way through green jungle and rice paddy fields. We passed the Sikkim border check post, and across endless little streams tumbling over the road which Nepali crews were manually repairing.

Then we wound back and forth, up and on until we reached Gangtok.

Before settling in at the government guest house, we visited Miss Patterson, the only European missionary working in Sikkim, and delivered her order of Darjeeling vegetables and Nepali Christian literature. She handed us neat white cards printed in blue, an official invitation from the Maharajah to attend the monastery dances and to be his luncheon guests.

The next day, we made our way to the top of the hill and the palace grounds. We found the local folk decked out in their brightest.

Ornately decorated, the monastery faced a low pavilion with a pagoda-like curved roof. Between the two buildings lay a neat lawn and a circular path, the stage for the Buddhist lamas' dance.

We were ushered through the dense crowd to the Maharajah's ornately decorated tent, where His Highness rose to greet us. Soon we were comfortably seated among other guests and our eyes were drawn to the "warrior dance."

From the pavilion, the clash of cymbals and the beat of a big dull drum announced each lama dancer as he slowly swung his way from the curtained entrance of the monastery onto the circular pathway. Only the tips of the ten-foot-long horns were visible through which the lamas produced deep prolonged tones. The dancers, attired in fanciful masks, embroidered red boots, and robes of silk and rich brocade, clasped long swords and minute shields. With slow, determined steps, they made wide sweeps, depicting warfare with the evil spirits. The crash of the cymbals and the dull blare of the horns played a steady background for the drama. It was anything but joyful.

We were seeing the pageantry of another world. This was a part of Buddhism in Sikkim, a worship of mountains and the demonic spirits believed to dwell there. Our hearts yearned that these whom God created might give Him alone the glory and honor due to Him.

At 1 p.m. we strolled over to a much larger tent where we were luncheon guests of His Highness. Delicious *palau*, (an Indian fried rice

Alma and Miss Patterson, and the whole Hagen family, were guests of Maharaja Tashi Namgyal of Sikkim.

dish), curries, nuts, and sweets were served in elegant buffet style. While we were eating, Kenny introduced himself to Hope Cook, another American guest at the festivities, dressed in a cotton dirndl and simple thongs. Kenny invited her to our home when she came to Darjeeling, never dreaming that she would one day be the *Gyalmo* or Queen of Sikkim.

That evening we were Miss Patterson's guests. We showed colored Bible slides to her dormitory girls. Then we returned to the government guest bungalow, eagerly anticipating the next day.

We had often heard of the enthusiastic, live group of Christians in Gangtok. We soon found they lived up to their name.

The brown, tiered-roof church lay nestled against a steep hillside. Uniquely Sikkimese in its architecture, the church with its cross stood a silent testimony to the surrounding Buddhist-Hindu environment. But the congregation was anything but a silent testimony. The church was packed. The unaccompanied singing rang out in joyous full tones.

More than a third of the 150 literate Christian families in the Gangtok area subscribed to our Nepali Christian magazine. As we joined those folk in praise and worship, we rejoiced to know that the true eternal God, who created Kanchenjunga and all the beauty, was being lifted up in this land. That afternoon an eager group of fifty young people gathered for the fellowship hour and a word from the visiting missionary.

The next day we packed up to go back to Darjeeling, never dreaming it might be our last.

As we started downhill, we reminisced of the picturesque scenes of Gangtok. Frequently we broke into choruses and songs. Roy drove along the road that followed high above the Tista, a river boiling and eddying in muddy swirls like so much coffee.

Suddenly, we saw two young men, dressed in white long-skirted South Indian attire, standing in the middle of the road waving frantically for us to stop. Roy quickly stopped. The men drew our attention to a narrow crack in the road forming a big semicircle some hundred feet long. At the immediate left edge of the road a steep cliff vaulted high above us. The right edge dropped straight down to the raging Tista river.

We debated, "Should we drive over?"

"No, no! You must not go!" they pleaded above the roar of the river. And then they showed us that dirt from behind the retaining wall, supporting the road, was pouring out at the bottom of the wall, right into the swirling torrent below. A bend in the swift monsoon-filled river had undercut the retaining wall and road.

We stood numb with horror as the crack widened. The road's edge, with its concrete barriers, then collapsed into the river. The retaining wall began breaking up into huge chunks that rumbled into the torrent below. With sickening swiftness, the whole section of the road disappeared into the vicious river. Where there had been a complete road fifteen minutes before, there was now only a yawning abyss.

If the road went out so suddenly of its own accord, what would have happened had our jeep with eight passengers driven over? It would have been sure death for us all.

Warned, and by God's miraculous grace, we were delivered from a watery grave.

We eventually found a tiny alternative tea-plantation road that we could take to leave Sikkim. It was barely passable by four-wheel-drive

On the way home, Hagens were stopped from crossing this section of the main road from Sikkim. Moments later, the road slid into the raging Tista River. This photo captures the landslide in progress.

jeeps. Part of the road had been built for mule trains to Tibet. The gateway to one bridge was so narrow we had to remove the spare tire on the side of the jeep in order to squeeze onto the bridge.

All of us got out of the jeep while Roy inched across that fragile bridge. Later we were told of a bridge in northern Sikkim that gave way, hurling forty-two people into the river to their death. This back road was very narrow, rough and steep, but the scenery was breathtakingly beautiful. We thanked the Lord for the privilege of seeing His magnificent handiwork.

Yes, we had visited a Maharajah, and we had witnessed color and pageantry. Far greater was the fact that the true God of all "Snowy Ranges" had saved us from a dreadful death for His further purposes. We were to continue warning those living under the "Snowy Ranges" of a more deadly slide into spiritual death, and of the narrow way to abundant life Jesus made through His sacrificial death on the cross. We must continue to stand at the brink, warning those hurrying along life's highway.

I took pictures of the road as it was giving way in front of us. Seeing two South Indians dressed in their usual white long-skirted attire commanding us to stop had truly gotten our attention. Sikkim just didn't have dark South-Indian men walking about in their long skirt-like costumes. Had it been two local Nepalis, we might not have paid such serious attention. When the film was developed, we saw only Nepalis on the other side of the huge break in the road! Did the Lord send angels to warn and protect us? I believe He did. That was not our last trip to Sikkim's palace.

To the Palace

Several years later we received an invitation from Her Highness, the Gyalmo herself. She had invited Ruth Heflin, Susan Woodaman and me for lunch. Susan and Hope had attended the same private girls' school.

I was delegated to drive. The Dalai Lama's sister-in-law and I were reknowned as the only women drivers in Darjeeling District! Ruth was decked out in a basic black dress. Susan wore red while I wore a soft blue sari. We safely crossed the Tista River and began the slow climb to the palace in Gangtok.

Then we met a convoy of Indian military trucks blocking the road. (The small state of Sikkim was a "protectorate" of India.) We stopped and waited patiently but nothing moved. Honking the horn would be unsuitable and useless. Smartly uniformed turbaned Sikh officers milled around the trucks. Ultimately, I realized I would have to talk to someone. Ruth and Susan prayed quietly for favor.

"Who is the Officer in Charge?" I casually asked one of the drivers. He directed me to the commanding Major. I timidly approached him and said, "Sir, we have an invitation to the palace for lunch and we simply must get through!"

"Yes Ma'am!" he declared, saluting me, and promptly ordered his drivers to move their vehicles to make room for our jeep. We crept slowly past the convoy and wound our way up to the palace, arriving just in time for lunch.

Ruth and Susan were surprised to see that the palace was patterned after an English-style country home. But inside, there were rich

East meets west at the palace in Sikkim. Alma in a sari, Ruth Heflin, the Gyalmo of Sikkim (nee Hope Cooke), and Susan Woodaman.

tapestries of Tibetan religious wall-hangings called *tankas* and beautiful Tibetan carpets.

The Gyalmo met us with her gracious soft-spoken whisper. The four of us sat around a low table. We were enthralled at the striking paintings decorating the room. But more importantly, we shared with Her Hightness Hope our life and joy in knowing the King of Kings.

Previously, the Gyalmo had invited all six of us to the coronation. Our sons had managed to stand on the very front row, not missing a thing. As she passed in the procession, the Gyalmo greeted Kenny. His feet hardly touched ground the rest of the day!

Fortunately, none of our future trips necessitated moving a military convoy, but we had much to learn about the necessity of spiritual warfare! I, for one, would learn some things about spiritual warfare that I had not expected.

Chapter 7

Taken by Surprise!

School of Discipleship

Some people seem to think that a missionary spends most of his time preaching to crowds thirsting for the Light. But much more common is ministering to folk who come to the door for help. However, the folk who come aren't always aware of their spiritual need.

Much else was in store for this missionary, including going to school. That was my lot for many weeks and months, — further training in a very private school, with the Master Himself as my Teacher.

My enrollment began when an abnormal electrocardiogram prompted our Doctor Meg to prescribe flat bedrest for one month, no visitors. Glandular fever had left me with a weakened heart. Perhaps in the Lord's eye, enrollment began before the cardiogram when I prayed, "Lord, break me and mold me, and make me what You want me to be."

To make sure I actually got the rest, Dr. Meg ordered me to bed in her own home, not mine. At first it felt good to rest, to sleep, and to just feed on the Word, after hectic busy weeks in the Mission House. God gave His pupil the word written of Noah, "The Lord shut him in…God remembered Noah."[21] I knew He was shutting me in, but that He remembered me, and my heart was at rest.

After ten days, though, I began flopping around in bed like a fish thrown up on the sand. "What about our four lively boys? Roy can't do everything—take care of them, do the work, and visit me! How long will I have to stay in bed? Isn't there some medicine that could give the same remedy as rest?" My thoughts tumbled in wild confusion.

Then one morning my eye caught this word: "Don't wrestle, just nestle."

That message was clearly for me. I confessed my restlessness.

---

[21] Gen.7:16; 8:1

The day I prayed, "Lord, break me and mold me," I had given afresh every ambition, my whole life to Him again as a love offering.

One morning, lying in my "classroom," I read, "If you bring your gift to the altar, and there you remember that your brother has ought against you, leave your gift. . . and go…first be reconciled to your brother…"[22] There was one close Nepali sister who I knew had "ought" against me. I had to admonish her one day, but I didn't do it in Calvary love and the Lord reminded me of that. My Teacher gave me a writing assignment, a letter asking forgiveness for my unloving spirit.

One quiet Sunday evening Roy came, sat on my bed and pulled a pink cable from his pocket. Word had just come half way around the world that my little mother had been promoted into her Savior's presence. My loving Teacher gently spoke to me of the fullness of joy in His presence, of the victory that now was Momsey's because of His resurrection. I was reminded of one of Momsey's many poems:

MOTHER LOVE

A memory of girlhood
Will haunt me evermore;
My deep-eyed little mother
Before the cottage door,
Her arm outstretched to greet me,
Glad welcome in her eye,
As tenderly she whispers,
"Who loves you more than I?"

Another memory picture:
One evening we alone
Beneath the stars, while softly
The summer breezes moan.
My arm clasped gently 'round her,
We sit there, eye in eye,
And now again she whispers,
"Who loves you more than I?"

---

[22] Matthew 5:23-24

Today that mother's waiting,
All glorified, tear-free,
Beyond the heavenly portals,
In far eternity.
The same devoted glances,
That loyal mother eye,
And now she seems to whisper,
GOD loves you more than I!"

Frieda Martini Buchen

A pastor, who had been used in healing sick folk by the laying on of hands, came and prayed for me. The Lord had given me promises of healing. I knew God was able to heal in a moment. After that laying on of hands, pains were less severe—but still persisted, and the good Teacher reminded, "Do you want Me as much as you want healing, My child? My ways are not your ways!"

After three weeks without visitors except my family, the doctor gave permission to call some close friends whom I had been eager to see. Word came back that they were unable to come.

Lying on the horizontal I had lots of time to think. "Christmas in less than two months! I'm sure that Dr. Meg will let me be back home—and even if I can't do much, our family will be together, and we'll have a tree and a happy time with the children around the fireplace!" I was full of eager anticipation.

Before Meg left for the hospital one morning, she came in for a chat. "No matter how much improvement your next cardiogram shows, you must get down to the plains as soon as you can arrange it, Alma. The cold and high altitude dilate the vessels." I hardly heard the rest. I fought a lump in my throat until Meg closed the door behind her.

"But Lord, Martha and Shilling are coming to spend their vacation with us….and Jonathan Maraj is coming, and I had planned a happy Christmas with all of us together!"

I realized my strong will was not broken and wholly His. It hurt to realize how I grieved the Lord with my stubbornness, and I said, "Lord, Your will!"

Through tears as I read from Amy Carmichael's *Gold by Moonlight,* the first sentence caught my eye, "The Father trusts His broken child to trust!" Another word: "This that has come to pass could not have been had it not been allowed. Then love allowed it!" and I whispered, "Thank You, Lord."

Weeks before I went to bed, an alcoholic had been coming to our home almost daily. One day he gave his heart to the Lord. Later he wrote what a changed person he was. His old gin bottle now served as a flower vase. But unbelieving friends said, "It won't last."

A month after his change I told a friend, "You should see Hoppy! He's a transformed person…" That same evening there was a tap at the door. Hoppy stepped in. One look and I knew he had been drinking again! I was numb with disappointment. In the quietness of the long night the Lord reminded me that He was teaching me to glory in Himself alone, not in fruit, or blessings, or individuals.

Then the Teacher gave me a questionnaire:

> O Thou beloved child of My desire,
> Whether I lead thee through green valleys,
> By still waters,
> Or through fire,
> Or lay thee down in silence under snow,
> Through any weather, and whatever
> Cloud may gather,
> Wind may blow –
> Wilt love Me? Trust Me? Praise Me?
>
> *Amy Carmichael* [23]

Then the Teacher gave me a ministry assignment appropriate to my strength. In between bringing me meals and dusting the room, the waiter in the doctor's home told of his little boy's dying of meningitis a few months before. The waiter, who had no hope after death, was bitter. The Lord had a consoling word for him. The lady who cared for Dr. Meg's little boy was alone in supporting herself and her only child. I had often wished for an opportunity to visit with her and share Jesus. She and I had many talks about spiritual things. The nurse, who came daily to care for me, had heavy burdens. Each had a need, and for every need Jesus had a word of life and hope.

When Mount Hermon School was out the end of November the boys and I headed for the warm plains. Roy followed in time for Christmas. We missed Shilling and Manu, but I was determined to

---

[23] Amy Carmichael, *Gold by Moonlight*, London: SPCK, 1935, 6th ed., 1943.

recover.

This missionary wasn't doing what folk in the homeland probably envisioned me to be doing. God was more concerned with who I was than what I did. He ministers in strange ways to His children. Only in eternity will we understand wholly God's plan and purpose. But in the meantime, I was sure I was where God in His love had permitted me to be. School was still in session.

It continued, even through a foreign invasion.

Invasion

October 20, 1962, was a day we would never forget. China invaded India! The Chinese poured over the northern border into the North East Frontier Area (NEFA) near Burma in the East and into Ladakh near Kashmir and Pakistan in the West. They burst through token resistance and swiftly reached the plains.

With only a few hours notice, fifteen hundred Britishers and two hundred Americans were ordered to evacuate from Assam, a comparatively short distance east of us. Having outrun their own supply lines, the Chinese agreed to a cease-fire.

Some ten thousand Chinese soldiers were still encamped on the Sikkim-China border at the strategic Nathu La Pass just eighty miles north of us. Our good friend George Patterson, Dr. Meg's husband, had accurately predicted this conflict in the face of Nehru and Chou En-Lai's eager friendship. His publisher said that *Peking versus Delhi* was the only book on India and China that was banned in both capitals![24] George had incredibly crossed the Himalayas in the dead of winter to carry Tibet's desperate plea for help from Lhasa to New Delhi.[25]

Just south of us, a narrow neck of India, fifteen miles wide, connected Assam and NEFA with the rest of India. That constriction contained the strategic rail junction and airport at Siliguri. If the Chinese army to our north broke through to that vital area, then Assam, an important source of oil and rice for all India, would be cut off. There was only one "major" road from Darjeeling to Siliguri. If that narrow

---

[24] George N. Patterson, *Peking versus Delhi,* Faber and Faber, London, 1963.

[25] George N. Patterson, *Patterson of Tibet*, ProMotion Publishing, San Diego, CA 92122, 1998.

winding road were blocked, it would be very difficult for us to evacuate Darjeeling.

A total wartime blackout was ordered for Darjeeling. Windows were covered, and the top half of headlights painted black. The military commandeered most vehicles to move troops to the border. The seven major boarding schools closed early and made emergency travel arrangements to transport thousands of students to their homes. Neighbors started digging trenches. Our boys pretended to fight invaders behind every tree.

We did our best to stick with witnessing. We had signed a government-issued paper saying we would stay out of politics, and in fact, I was quite naive about many political matters. During 1962, a local rebel strongly influenced by the Communists, started badgering me, "You are CIA, aren't you?" "Of course not." I replied, not really knowing what CIA meant. After he pestered me for six months, I finally said in exasperation "Do you know what CIA stands for?" "No," he said. I replied, "It means 'Come In Again.' Any time you want, you can Come In Again. Sure I am CIA."

The next week the Darjeeling newspaper reported that I was a CIA suspect. A friend in India's Central Intelligence Department later told us that our files now stated we were self proclaimed CIA agents and were known to be broadcasting into India! Later we learned what CIA meant and discovered that people have been killed after their names were published as suspect CIA agents. I was learning that folk of another culture did not always understand our form of American humor. I also learned, the hard way, not to even joke about political involvement. Mercifully, we were protected from harm in that highly charged atmosphere.

Early one morning in November, I stood outside watching the sunrise tint Mt. Kanchenjunga with vibrant rose and then gold. The gong sounded in the Hindu temple below. Its bells tinkled. The Hindu worshipers were informing their gods that they had prayed. Very quietly but clearly, our Lord spoke to me, "Take the boys home and put them in American schools."

Our five-year furlough was due in April. Roy and I talked it over and prayed together, committing the whole matter into our Father's hands. With the war, Darjeeling schools might not open in the spring. Then if we returned to the States on schedule in the summer, our four boys would be out of school for ten months. We needed approval from our fellow workers for the children and me to leave early. Permission was given readily. Roy would stay behind until the next summer.

If the boys and I left before Paul's twelfth birthday February 17, we would save $375 by his not needing an adult ticket. Only Roy and I knew that we were still short $600 in travel funds to pay for all the tickets. All our travel expenses had to be paid from personal gifts apart from Mission funds. We didn't tell another soul of our need.

We sent a letter off to the World Mission Prayer League office at the end of November telling of our field's approval for my taking the boys home early. Before our letter reached Minneapolis, the monthly accounts were closed at the end of November. WMPL's monthly financial statement and checks crossed our letter in the mail. In the November list of gifts was a $600 gift specially earmarked "for travel for Hagens." Thank You, Father!

I would soon thank the Lord for a special pair of earrings.

Blue Earrings and Crutches

As our four boys and I flew back to the States we had a stop over in Germany, visiting my second cousin, Herta Putz, and her two children, Siegfried and Ursula. Herta's deacon husband had been taken captive by the Russians during World War II when her children were tiny. In hopes that he would someday return, she had never declared him dead, foregoing her right to a widow's pension. (Years later she learned that he died in a Czechoslovakian prisoner of war camp.)

Snuggling under big feather beds was great fun for four peppy boys. But how to keep them quiet when they all woke up at four a.m., raring to go, their bodies still on Indian time? The joys of jet travel!

We visited the town of Buchen, which my father said was named after his family. However, we found no trace of a baronial home. The photos he had shown us were of a private school!

Though arrangements had been made for the boys and me to stay at the WMPL Mission Home, the apartment assigned to us had not yet been vacated, so Roy's parents graciously opened their home to us.

It was a big adjustment for all of us. Four lively boys suddenly made an unbelievable difference in their home. I was tense. The boys needed leeway to "be boys," but there had to be enforced boundaries.

Compassionate nine-year-old Kenny sensed my tension. One

evening he disappeared just before supper. Soon he returned clutching a tiny package in his fist. He had taken his week's allowance and gone to the nearby drugstore. When he opened his package, he handed me a pair of lovely blue earrings.

"I wanted to get you some nice white flowers that had MOTHER in gold letters, but the store lady thought you would like these better." (Little Kenny had no experience with American style funerals or funeral wreaths.) I was consoled and comforted by such a loving, thoughtful gift.

Then came a spring weekend on an American farm! Art and Nora Haukvik invited us to their farm near Hanska, Minnesota. I had lived with them the summer I taught their children in vacation Bible school. There would be tractors and all kinds of animals, new things to see and learn—and give Grandpa Chris and Grandma Ingeborg a needed break!

One morning after breakfast, Nora and I lingered over a cup of coffee, sharing the goodness of the Lord. Suddenly Paul dashed into the kitchen, white as a sheet.

"Mommy, Kenny hurt his leg real bad!" Paul tore back out the door and I followed as fast as I could.

Kenny had been watching the silage of ground corn coming down out of the tall silo through a chute into a large trough. An auger pushed the silage to the far end of the trough, where the cows fed on it. Kenny had been standing on the two sides of the trough. Suddenly his leg had slipped into the trough, jamming the huge screw-like feed auger.

"Dear Jesus, help me get my leg out! Dear Jesus, help me get my leg out!" he screamed, calling to his real source of help.

Art ran to turn off the auger. Then he worked feverishly to take the trough apart to get Kenny's leg out. We all called on the Lord for His help and mercy. Nora phoned the doctor in nearby Madelia, who arrived just as we got Kenny's leg freed from the trough. The doctor rushed Kenny the forty miles to Mankato Hospital. There Dr. D.C. Meredith, one of the outstanding orthopedic surgeons in Minnesota, had the operating room prepared for him. I waited anxiously while Kenny was in surgery. The Madelia doctor had told of two other boys who had lost a leg in a similar accident. I took comfort from Psalm 34:19-20 "A righteous man may have many troubles, but the Lord delivers him from them all. He protects all his bones, not one will be broken."

When Dr. Meredith finally appeared, he said, "We saved his leg but Ken probably won't walk normally again." Kenny came out from under anesthesia singing, "The Lord's my shepherd, I'll not want." He required six further trips to the operating room to have large skin grafts done. One day while receiving a blood transfusion and realizing how important blood transfusions were for his recovery, he looked up at the blood dripping into his arm and said, "And to think that Jesus gave His blood for me!"

My first cable to Roy telling of the accident didn't reach him. The second one saying that Ken would be able to walk was the first news

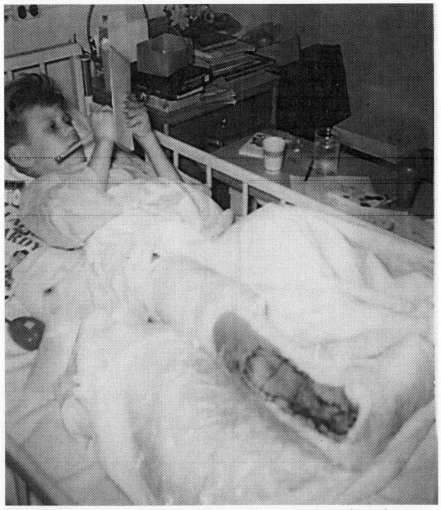

Ken's slip into the auger during a visit to an American farm nearly cost him his leg.

to reach him. The mercies of God!

A large cast was applied from Kenny's thigh to his toes. When the cast ultimately came off a month later, we put him in a tub of warm water and pushed his stiff knee down a thousand times twice a day. Three months later when he could leave crutches behind, Kenny's walk was perfectly normal. Though the peroneal tendon had been destroyed, adhesions had corrected what the doctor felt would be abnormal.

The news of a nine-year-old missionary boy from India having an accident in an auger feeder was broadcast over the rural radio system. Sunday Schools, churches and individuals sent books, puzzles, toys and cash. Miraculously all the medical bills were paid. God's mercies were boundless. Truly he delivered Kenny "out of them all."

Kenny's leg healed so completely that years later at Augsburg College he was chosen the "soccer goalie" of Minnesota.

Left behind in India, Roy found that the nuisance of blackouts could be overcome.

Chapter 8

New Life

Bringing Light to Darkness

The blackouts and threatened invasion didn't stop the light from going forth.

During the Festival of Lights, all the Hindu folk sweep their homes carefully and string garlands of orange marigold flowers over windows and doorways. In the evenings, they normally light tiny oil lamps placed in windows and the courtyard in hopes of pleasing Lakshmi, the goddess of wealth.

One day during that festival, Roy went back to the Bible school to encourage the students in literature distribution. They filled their bags with Gospels, and squeezed into the jeep. Then Roy drove from Mirik to Kalimpong. The team visited some of the elders of the United

NISS Staff, L.B. Rai and B.B. Subba, prepared manuscripts for publishing and tracked finances.

Church of North India to work out plans for distributing Gospels and tracts.

The atmosphere among the elders was one of dark fear. They were cautious about causing any disturbance. But after prayer, great peace filled the room. Everyone agreed that this was exactly what the Lord, the Prince of Peace, had sent them to do.

Instead of literature distribution causing a riot, as the locals feared, the people gladly received the joyful messages of hope and God's Word. The entire supply of literature was gone by the following noon, and the team returned to Mirik.

It was a strange Festival of Lights. Every house was swept clean inside and out. However, there were no lights burning because of the military blackout. The real light came from the Lord. It was seen in

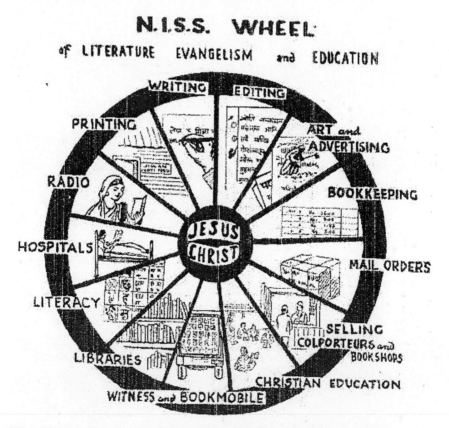

The Nepali Christian Literature Society declared Jesus to be the hub of the vision for sharing Christ through many avenues.

those witnessing and in those receiving the Gospel. Light overcame darkness.

Christian literature was a long arm reaching out to far more people than Christians could witness to personally, or reach through the traditional costly institutions. A missionary in Nepal wrote Roy, "When you organize your distribution work, think big. Within Nepal, literature distribution is our number one means of proclaiming the Gospel…I am not thinking of a few hundred copies of each title, but tens of thousands. Among fourteen million Nepali-speaking people this is not unrealistic if we are good salesmen."

In the decade since we first arrived in India in 1951, a million Nepalis had learned to read. Our literature arm would bring them light all across "Himalasia," the Himalayan countries where Nepalis live: Nepal, Sikkim, Bhutan and north India.

We prayed for a printer to oversee the more complicated printing. The Lord wonderfully answered prayer and sent a journeyman printer, Carl Zimmerman, and his wife Ruby. Budhiman continued working for JJP, Jiwan Jyoti Prakashan, (Light of Life Press).

We prayed for a building to house the NISS publishing program.

Roy was happy to be standing in front of the the newly built, much needed Nepali Christian Literature Society (NISS) building.

A site was chosen directly uphill from the Scots Mission House. Because nearly everything in Darjeeling was built on a hill, eight-foot reinforced concrete pillars below the ground were needed to support the foundation. The twenty-eight feet by forty eight feet building came to $4,000. It was situated along one of Darjeeling's main roads and accessible to motor vehicles. This gave a good opportunity to display books, contact the public, and bring supplies right to the door. The new JJP building was dedicated to God on April 13, 1963. Since the press had not yet moved into the building there was room for a hundred people to attend the dedication. Our blind Nepali friend, Birendra, played classical Indian sitar music. KP Bhattarai, a recent Brahmin convert, translated and chanted his "Hymn of Love." Jonathan Thapa, who had completed college and was being trained by Carl Zimmerman for press management, sang scripture messages set to popular Nepali folk tunes. It was a joyous day. That little building would be a center for spreading the Gospel far and wide.

The NISS had become recognized as Nepali Publishers by all those working among Nepalis and by the Government of India as one of its registered societies. The NISS staff consisted of three nationals and two missionaries. It had produced and distributed a monthly and a quarterly magazine, eighteen tracts, and forty books and booklets—all since it was formed in September, 1960. The flat missionaries were spreading the light.

Roy left to join us in the States for a well-deserved furlough, but while we were in America, we would receive totally unexpected news from India.

Shilling's Promotion

Just before Christmas, 1963, Shilling, Martha, three-year-old David and baby Suzanne traveled to Darjeeling for a refreshing break. They had to take a strenuous hike of six days through the hills before reaching public transport.

One day Martha wanted to buy new clothes for Shilling. "I won't need any!" he replied. Several times that day he and Martha prayed together. "Isn't it wonderful that God never dies!" he declared. That night Father God called Shilling to his heavenly home. Shilling had lived faithfully unto the Lord. He had continued to live "not I but

Christ."

At his funeral, Martha gave a courageous testimony of God's call to them to minister in Nepal. That call had not changed even though she returned with two small children and without Shilling. The Lord had promised her in Psalm 146:9, "The Lord . . . sustains the fatherless and the widow." That was enough. She knew her Lord Jesus was faithful!

Martha continued serving the Lord. In Kathmandu, she became the headmistress of Mahendra Bhawan, Nepal's first high school for girls. This school soon gained a reputation for its academic excellence. But it had begun as a kindergarten with dirt floors that the teacher regularly plastered with fresh mud. The one instructor not only cooked for the children, but bathed and dressed them. As the children grew older, they learned by the teacher's example. Reflecting on the changes that occurred during her years as a teacher at Mahendra Bhawan, Mrs. Shrestha wrote:

> *"Some of the students in the hostel came from higher caste families. They would not even put away their plates after meals. But later they began to wash the dishes. They started to cook, wash and do all kinds of work. The students became capable of many aspects of life. Today some of those students are teachers at Mahendra Bhawan and other schools, some are doctors and nurses, some are engineers and professors. Many have become good, capable housewives."[26]*

Later, Martha taught at the UMN Gandaki Boarding School in Pokhara. This school, too, was known for its high standards. Many of its graduates have held high positions in government.

Reviewing Shilling's life in Nepal, Jonathan Lindell wrote:

> *"Shilling wasn't a 'great' person . . . The thing that is valuable and important is that during his seven years in Nepal he was a **mature** Christian missionary. Mature in that he went himself and strengthened himself in the Lord . . . He was a source of help, advice, concern, guidance to others, to*

---

[26] Mrs. Dhana Shrestha, *The Hostel Duty of Mahendra Bhawan School*, UMN News, No. 16, 6-7, March 2004.

many, many school boys, to village men, to patients, to needy people. This is in contrast to the many Christian workers . . . who never grow up to that degree.

*"Then he was a **genuine** Christian. He had his religion out of his own thorough and continuing study of the Bible and daily meeting with Christ. He didn't live by the spiritual propping or feeding of others . . . He walked on his own feet with the Lord, taking correction, conviction, confession, forgiveness, renewing, joy, peace, hope, sanctification direct from the Holy Spirit. Because of this he was a father, a leader, a pillar, a supporting member of the Church.*

*"Then he was a **true** missionary. He had a real calling from God to leave his home and people and possessions and ways of life and go into Nepal to give himself in the service of the Lord. This meant that his viewpoint and attitude toward everything was different. His attitude toward salary, money, housing, use of his time, use of his goods, his work, his family, his colleagues, his neighbors was colored and slanted by this missionary outlook. He didn't have an employee complex, i.e., he didn't consider himself basically an employee of a mission to serve his appointed hours of work to please his employer . . . but his basic attitude was that he was a member of a team of persons sent by God to do a job for the people of the community . . . He thought and talked missionary aims, principles, practices, problems . . . He applied himself to the missionary job as a 24- hour job with joy, prayer, work, concern, in order to get his God-given job done. This meant you could work with him as a brother."*[27]

We would miss Shilling as one misses a member of the family, but we had the quiet assurance that we would meet again in our heavenly home. A high-positioned older man with a long white beard would want to join that family.

---

[27] Jonathan Lindell, *World Vision*, May, p.7, 1964.

"Get Me That Book!"

Why is Christian literature so important? Let me tell you a story from the records of the American Bible Society that Carl Zimmerman, our printer, read to us.

"I was a Christian man, living in India, a surveyor in the employ of the Government, and was sent to survey the desert of Rajputana in the Northwest.

"I entered the desert with the necessary accouterments. When night came...I invited the villagers to my tent. (They knew I was a government official and they thought that perhaps I had a government message for them.)

"When the time came I stepped out of the tent, and there were the people. There was the great silvery moon, dropping such light as is seen nowhere else than in the tropics. I stood and looked out on that company and was strangely moved...I was 180 miles away from any town in any direction. I suppose my thought was absolutely true that those who were listening to me had probably never once heard the name of Jesus Christ. Let me say that there is a certain high tension of spirit, a certain sense of tremendous responsibility, accompanied with a certain profound gladness, when you feel that those who are listening are absolutely hungry, famine-stricken without the Word of God.

"I talked to those men that night. I spoke their language. At the close of that earnest and perhaps somewhat long address—who could help it? — this happened:

"An old man came forward. He was the son of a king, his long beard flowing down to his waist. He came up to me, leaning on his staff. The young men courteously made way for him. He stood there looking up at me, his strong face alert in that bright moonlight. He said: 'You are a young man, and yet the things you have been talking about—how do you know these things? How do you know them?'

"I answered, 'Father, I have not known these things because of my own personal righteousness or wisdom. But these questions which have troubled your heart and all human hearts, our Great Father has written down in a Book,

given to men of olden time who struggled with these questions. And the answers to these questions were written in a Book.'

"'Do you mean there is a book with all these things you have been telling us about—about a love that is good, and all the rest of it?'

"Then I said, 'There is a Book. It is God's Book, and the answers are in it.'

"'Young man,' said he, 'is that book in my language? You speak my language. Did you read it in my tongue?'

"'Yes, I have the Book.'

"I wish you could have seen that old man. He straightened up and pointed his long finger at me (I shall never forget it) as he said: 'Get me that book!'

"I ran back to my tent and brought back two copies of the Bible in their language. Forty brown hands were stretched out for them as I returned. I put one into his hand, and when I told him that the answers to the questions were in that Book, the old man looked up and said, 'Sir, how long has this book been in the world?'

"'It has been here for hundreds of years.'

"'Did your people have it?'

"'Yes.'

*"'And I am an old man. All my friends have died hopeless. I am nearly gone myself. And all this time the book was here and nobody brought it to me. **Why didn't someone bring us the book long ago?'"***

The Lord Himself had instructed us to publish glad tidings. We had a mandate to go and tell. Not only were we to translate, and distribute the Word of God, but there were hearts open and hungry for even a small portion of the Word.

Another old man of a renowned family would help us translate that precious Word.

Colonel Sahib

When Roy was assigned to "literature work and Bible Translation" in 1957 he joined the team of men working on the revision of the Nepali New Testament to get "That Book" to the Nepalis. The Bible Society of India and Ceylon had started that revision in 1954. The Church of Scotland provided Rev. H. E. Duncan, and then Rev. James Brodie.

To produce a translation that would be acceptable inside Nepal as well as outside required someone from within the land to join the team. Nepali spoken in Darjeeling differed from that spoken in Kathmandu, Nepal. The principal and a teacher from Darjeeling's Turnbull Boy's High School, Mahendra Kumar and Hem Chendra Pradhan, and Dharmadan Pradhan, teacher from Mirik High School, were native speaking scholars and represented Darjeeling Nepali. The Bible Society engaged "Colonel Sahib" to represent Kathmandu Nepali.

He was a charming frail little man with a big handlebar mustache. Very quiet by nature, he had a soft lisp as though breathing in air through his mouth. He wore his Nepali cap and was never without his accompanying servant, except when translating.

Hem Chandra Pradhan and the Colonel Sahib translating the Scriptures.

Then Nepal's Door Opened

Officially known as Colonel Nararaj Shamshere Jung Bahadur Rana, he told us his story. Born August 15, 1896, he was the grandson of Bir Shamshere, Nepal's prime minister from 1885-1901. One of fifteen brothers and twelve sisters, the Colonel lived with his grandmother in her famous *Lal Durbar* (Red Palace) until he was sixteen. Then he finally went to live with his father and stayed there until he was twenty-three. Colonel Sahib married several wives, not an uncommon practice among Ranas in Nepal.

At twenty he had made his first trip to India to take his Matric high school exams in Calcutta. Of that trip he said, "The big shops in Calcutta impressed me the most. I used to be very interested in perfumes and bought different scents. In Calcutta, the English walked on one side of the sidewalk, the Bengalis on the other. I liked the English and their discipline."

He began his military training at seventeen and continued until he was thirty-six. He continued:

"I became a Colonel of the Nepal Army. My father was the Commanding General and now Field Marshall. I became the Governor of Dhankuta for two years. I don't like hilly places. I am afraid of the mountains. I still felt as though I was in prison while in Kathmandu, surrounded by mountains.

"When I passed through Raxaul en route to Dhankuta in 1932, some white man presented me with an English New Testament. I read only a few pages.

"There was a lot of puja (worship) in my life. We went from temple to temple. I had no idea of sins. I used to think that the very idols I worshiped would give me everything. In the temples we threw money to the idols to gain their favor. The Brahmin priests read the Puran (Hindu scriptures). We had to give them money, food and clothing.

"I had no idea about my soul at all. I believed that if I died, my soul entered another body. I read and prayed many prayers written in Sanscrit, (the language in which ancient Hindu scriptures were written). I didn't know the meaning of the Sanscrit and to this day I don't know it."

"Because of some political quarrels in 1934, six families were banished from the capitol.

"We moved to Raniganj, three miles from the India

border. My daughter became very ill with jaundice and was sent to Raxaul hospital. I had never seen a hospital before. My father had his own doctor.

In 1938 I took my grandson to the same hospital. I stayed there twenty-two days with my grandson. Mr. Oliver came to Raxaul from Motihari, called me to the Dr. Sahib's bungalow and prayed for my grandson and told me about the Lord Jesus. On September 8, 1939, he presented me with an English Bible. In 1940 Mr. Oliver sent Scripture Union Notes. Then I could truly understand what is Christianity. After obtaining those notes, I gave up the practice of worshiping idols. Even now I use Scripture Union Notes.

"Mr. Oliver also gave me a copy of John's Gospel in English and one also in old Nepali and told me to translate it.

"First I was greatly interested in the Sermon on the Mount. I began to pray to Jesus after 1947-1949. Mr. Oliver suggested I read the New Bible Handbook *and* The Bible Comes Alive. *I read them thoroughly and they were a big help. I read* Death of Christ *by Denny, the best book I have found in my life. I went through it three or four times...what Christ's death means to us. I read my Bible, but behind closed doors.*

"After the Nepal revolution in 1950, when the Rana rule

Revising the Bible from outdated language to commonly understood Nepali took this translation team years for both the New Testament and the Old Testament.

*ended in Nepal, I was encouraged to be really open. After
1951 the Lord guided me to Kathmandu again. The Roman
Catholics entered Nepal that year.*
      "In 1952 I requested Mr. Oliver to baptize me."

When the Colonel returned to Kathmandu, his first wife plus the
rest of his family attended South-Indian Sunday services in his home.
(He continued to support his other wives.) When four South-Indian
Mar Thoma believers came to Kathmandu in 1953, they found the
Colonel Sahib's home open to them. It was the beginning of a new
fellowship coming to Kathmandu.

As more Christians arrived in Nepal, they started and ran good
efficient hospitals and health services. No longer could the Colonel
Sahib say he had not seen a hospital in his country.

Roy and the translation committee had been working diligently.
By 1963 the New Testament and the Psalms had been revised by the
translation committee into much more up-to-date and easily understood
Nepali. The Nepali Bible translation team then proceeded with
updating the Old Testament. However, it had to do without Colonel
Sahib's able services as he was promoted to be with the Savior he
loved.

If there were to be more testimonies like the Colonel Sahib's, there
would need to be more Gospel literature, and that meant we needed a
bigger and better printing press.

Moving the Heidelberg

By hand-feeding the treadle printing press, we could barely print
a thousand sheets per hour. Although much better than the original tiny
hand clamshell press, it was still painfully slow considering the many
jobs waiting to be done.

"We need a bigger, better press!" Carl declared. So we earnestly
sought the Lord for a newer machine. Carl scouted around and found
a Heidelberg Press for sale in New Delhi. The owner was ready to sell.
Carl bought some lumber, found a good carpenter to help him, and the
two went to work making a shipping crate to ship the press from New
Delhi to Darjeeling.

The bigger challenge in New Delhi came when the crated press was ready to be loaded onto the truck by eight coolies. They were strong, but how were they to raise the big crate onto the truck? They wanted Carl to buy sweets to offer to one of their Hindu gods. Carl didn't feel free to do that, but he prayed in Jesus' name for help with the moving.

Soon the shipping agent came, bought the sweets and took them to a nearby shrine where he offered them to the Hindu god. He brought the sacrificed sweets back, placed them on the corners of the crate, and soon the men were willing to go to work. The coolies heaved and pushed and gradually the big crate was raised by a block and tackle onto the truck. Such are some of the challenges missionaries face as they struggle to witness for Christ in a pluralistic society.

Eight days later the New Delhi truck arrived in Darjeeling with the valuable crate. With no block and tackle available, Carl had to think through some clever engineering to get the Heidelberg off the truck and all the way into the NISS building. The men first dug a hole in the side

Moving the big Heidelberg Press into the NISS building took a big push and many helping hands.

of the hill for the truck to back into. The crate was then gradually slid off the truck onto rollers. Using the Mission jeep, the men pushed and pulled the crate until it was finally situated in the press building. What a relief.[28]

Now we could do first class work and print 16,000 pages an hour. But more than 16,000 pages were needed one midnight hour.

Midnight Emergency

Right at midnight there was a loud thump on Carl Zimmerman's door. When Carl opened the door, he was surprised to see Budhiman Rai, the JJP Printer.

"Please, older brother, come to my home and take my children to the hospital. I am afraid they are dying of food poisoning!" Carl jumped into the jeep, sped to Budhiman's home, got the whole family into the jeep and then raced through the empty streets. While careening around the corners, Carl reminded Budhiman and his wife that Jesus was their only hope and prayed, committing the little ones into His hands.

It was one-thirty a.m. when they finally arrived at the hospital. The doors were quickly unlocked, and miraculously, a doctor was on hand to attend to the five children, two of whom were already nearly unconscious.

The next day Carl was called again, this time to take the children home from the hospital. The Lord had indeed answered prayer. This spoke powerfully to Budhiman.

During the past ten years he had learned of Jesus through the Word he had printed as well as daily devotions in the Jiwan Jyoti Press. Many had witnessed to Budhiman. Folk had prayed faithfully for him. Now he was convinced that Jesus was the true God who died to save him from sin and who answered prayer.

The next week during Press devotions, the staff was singing, "I am coming to the Cross" when Budhiman began to weep. He interrupted the singing to say he wanted to share his testimony. He told of his new-found-faith in Jesus and what God had done for him. The staff hung on every word. Carl added his own personal testimony.

---

[28] Carl Zimmerman, *A Helper Arrives, Fellow Workers*, April, p. 2, 1966.

The day after Budhiman surrendered to Jesus, his wife Radhika also asked Jesus into her heart. The couple was now truly united in the Lord. Morning by morning Budhiman brought his Bible to work. He invited his Hindu neighbors to his home to hear the good news that he and Radhika had experienced. One day Budhiman asked for permission to leave work early to ask a friend's forgiveness for a wrong he had done in the past.

Soon the whole family was baptized. What a day of rejoicing that was. Both the Father in heaven and His angels were rejoicing with us.

Replaced with Growth

After the Heidelberg Press was installed, the literature program simply leaped forward. LEAP stood for Literacy and Education Advance Program. This program made a quarter of a million Nepali Christian books available throughout Nepal and the surrounding Nepali speaking communities. Forty-some folk volunteered to stock the books and recruit others to sell them.

We were continually reminded that missionaries might not be able to continue working in India, so Roy spent much of his effort in training Nepalis to take the leadership in literature. Staff members received excellent training in various seminars and institutes. L.B. Rai attended the International Publishers' Seminar in New York. Our editor, Arnold Rongong, went to a writer's course. Roy led the whole staff in a retreat at a Cinchona Plantation, focusing on Leadership in Nepali Christian Literature.

Well illustrated, graded Sunday School books for both teachers and pupils came off the press. One of the crowning events was the printing of *The Nepali Bhajan Sangrah* or hymn book. Ron Byatt had spent many long hours compiling the 450 most popular Nepali songs and hymns. Then he prepared the music scores. One copy was even purchased by a visitor from South India who introduced some of the tunes to her church. This hymn book was a wonderful contribution to the Nepali church. The core text is being reprinted and is still being used.

One special visitor in 1967 was Gwen Shaw (nee Schmidt) who asked us to print her tract *"Who is Jesus?"* in Nepali. Now forty years later we and the End-Time Handmaidens are still distributing that excellent tract.

In 1967, we published fifty books, a total of 246,000 copies, three periodicals resulting in 64,000 copies, and six tracts amounting to 120,000 copies. Hospitals and leprosariums in Nepal asked for literature, as did the newly opened schools. The little flat missionaries were traveling far and wide, over shaky rope bridges, from hand to hand, and by bus and land rover, and even by plane. Books and tracts were being sent to Nepal, Sikkim, Bhutan, parts of Assam, Burma, the Philippines, Taiwan and many spots in India. God had told us to write the vision and make it plain (Habakkuk 2:2) God's Word was going out! We rejoiced, even though an unexpected Britisher tried to stymie us![29]

"Winston Churchill" Steals the Jeep

With a turquoise dangling from his left ear, Joe[30] stuck a dagger between the two front seats. Tom,[31] another scruffy bearded unwashed hippie climbed in. Then they quietly backed the Jiwan Jyoti Prakashan press jeep away from the garage door where it was parked. Joe turned a crochet hook in the ignition and pushed down on the accelerator with his bare foot. Tom braced himself, and watched warily from behind his granny glasses as Joe sped down the crowded street.

But several of the publishing staff heard the jeep start up. Peering out of the front office they glimpsed the two hippies driving away. They dropped everything and took a short cut down the hill to try to cut them off.

Nepalis and Tibetans fled like chickens before a hawk as the jeep raced uncertainly down the narrow winding streets. One policeman nearly lost an arm as he tried to stop the thieves. Others stood numb as the jeep missed them by a hair.

Some weren't so fortunate. Two land rovers, filled with passengers, were sideswiped as the jeep careened around the corners.

---

[29] Roy Hagen, *Nepali Isai Sahitya Sangha, Fellow Workers*, Oct., pp.7-9, 1967.

[30] Not his real name.

[31] Not his real name.

The two damaged vehicles made straight for the Darjeeling Police Station.

In the middle of Ghoom market, four miles from Darjeeling, the hippies hit another jeep so badly it left the JJP jeep perpendicular across the road, its front jammed into a tiny shop.

Bearded Joe jumped out from behind the steering wheel and fled into the woods. Tom didn't fare so well. In the jolt of hitting another jeep and the shop, he struck his head on the windshield. Blood oozed and trickled down his forehead.

The hot fighting blood of the nearby Gurkhas rose up. Everyone could tell the impostor in the blue shirt and granny glasses had no business in a vehicle marked JIWAN JYOTI PRAKASHAN, a Nepali organization. They quickly surrounded Tom and dragged him down the road to the Ghoom police station.

In the meantime, Bible school teacher, Rebecca Rai, and I had come back to Mission House from an errand. Word of the jeep incident spread like wild fire, "Hippies have stolen the jeep!" Then we heard they had crashed in Ghoom. Rebecca and I hopped into our mission jeep and hurried out to Ghoom to see how badly they had damaged the JJP vehicle. We took a detective with us.

We made arrangements to bring the damaged jeep to the Darjeeling police station. I felt compelled to see this stranger, a prisoner in a foreign land. We were given permission to visit him.

He lay on a mat on the cement floor, behind heavy bars.

"Are you badly hurt?" I asked.

With a smirky snarl he cursed me with a volley of unprintable words.

"Jesus can help you much more than that jeep, brother! He came to set you free from this kind of life style. He loves you and He doesn't want you to live like this."

"Oh you filthy capitalist, coming out here to take advantage of Nepali people! Don't preach to me! ..." He went on to spout much more. The Lord gave me deep peace and a real pity for the fellow.

"What's your name?" asked the detective who had been listening to the whole conversation.

"Winston Churchill!" came the sassy reply. The officer looked at Tom's British passport.

A short while later Joe surrendered himself to the police. Then the two were taken to the Darjeeling jail.

A month later some of us felt constrained to visit the two prisoners. Permission was obtained from the District Magistrate. We took our permit, homemade brownies, sandwiches, two modern translations of the New Testament and Wilkerson's *The Cross and the Switchblade*. We wound our way down seven hundred feet to the very foot of Darjeeling.

Chains rattled and locks clicked open as our party of four entered through heavy creaking iron doors. The friendly warden received us most graciously in his office.

Soon the two appeared, clean-shaven. They greeted us coolly. We expressed our concern for them, prisoners in a strange environment. They seemed to appreciate the homemade food.

But New Testaments?

"I've read the Bible!" smirked Joe still wearing the one turquoise earring.

"You are searching for something, or you wouldn't be traveling around the world. When you meet Truth, who is Jesus Christ, your search will end. Read the New Testament. He will talk to you through it."

Then Theodore Manaen, one of our group, spoke up. In his gracious manner, he said, "You know, I was a prisoner here once for a political cause."

He then had Joe and Tom's rapt attention.

"Years ago I said 'no' to Jesus Christ," Theodore continued, "and I went to the top of politics in this country. I served there for many years." (He had been a Member of Parliament from Darjeeling District and rose to high leadership of the Congress Party). "But I had no peace. Then I came back to Jesus. I said, 'You save me, Lord. I yield to You,' Only then did I find peace. He washed away my sins, and I am a new person."

The prisoners hung on every word Theodore said. We had a short prayer for them and assured them of our continued prayers. Then we left.

We heard that the two had been sentenced to three months hard labor and transferred to a larger prison. Later we received a letter from "Winston Churchill."

New Life

Dear Mrs. Hagen:

Well, I guess you'll remember the event I was involved in at Darjeeling, the stealing of the jeep.

I'm writing to thank you for coming to see us in the jail and for the gift of the New Testament. It gave me great strength.

Also extreme apologies for my reception of you at the cell in Ghoom police station. Well, a little history since we last met.

After a month in Berhampur jail, a warm and welcome change from the cold of Darjeeling, we were released on the 2nd of December. I really felt lost in Calcutta and was ready for returning back to England.

Anyway, I didn't return and now I'm studying Zen Buddhism at this Ashram (An ashram in Bodh Gaya, a spiritual center where some believe Buddha received his enlightenment...)

By the way, I heard that Joe has returned to New Zealand.

Once again, thanks for your attention and for showing me something to have faith in. Still not sure of things but I feel I'm going in the right direction.

Regards,

Tom

Years later I received another letter from Tom written in England. This time he told of having received Jesus as His Savior, of surrendering his whole life to Him and what peace he had now found.

There was a new name written down in glory: Tom alias "Winston Churchill."

Chapter 9

The Bear Came Over the Mountain

About Jesus and His Daddy

Guests or not, when our four small boys finished their homework, we often huddled in front of the fireplace to read *Winnie the Pooh*, by A.A. Milne, or other children's stories.

One day our guests were Allen and Leoda Buckwalter, founder and directors of the Far East Broadcasting Associates of India. They overheard me reading "Pooh" to the boys and promptly begged me to make radio recordings for the English-speaking children of India. I had never recorded for radio in my life, but the idea "clicked." Since Winnie the Pooh was a bear, and we lived in the mountains, it was only natural that we were soon humming *The Bear Went Over the Mountain*, a popular children's song.

The transistor radio had become the source of news to rich and the poor, to the high and the low, to the city dweller and the scattered mountain farmers. It had opened the door to millions. It was a sure way to reach the most people in the shortest amount of time. And if you have something worth telling, you tell it. That was why Far East Broadcasting Association, FEBA, began.

We had something we not only wanted to tell but something we must tell. For the King of Kings had commanded us to go and to tell the world about Him and His love for all mankind. We were under orders from Jesus.

But why in English? Many children in grade school and high school were learning English.

When Dr. Meg ordered me to get away from the high altitude to the plains to recuperate, the Buckwalters invited me to Delhi to record. Thus began a fifteen-minute weekly children's program called *Treasure Hunt*. After the opening theme song, *The Bear Went Over the Mountain*, came the greeting, "*Treasure Hunt*, boys and girls! This is your Auntie Alma with another wonderful story just for you." A combination of classic children's stories and teaching about Jesus followed.

Little did we imagine how that innocent effort would later be misconstrued as alleged evidence of our supposed involvement as CIA agents known to be transmitting messages into India.

After that first recording stint in Delhi, I recorded in Calcutta, the closest studio to Darjeeling. That meant making all arrangements to leave a household humming with children and activities to travel four hundred miles south to record in the well-equipped studio of Rev. Mark Buntain.

I soon found out that Satan despises Christian radio work. He is the prince of the power of the air, and he does all he can to thwart God's message on the air. Even though we began each recording with prayer and claiming God's victory in the name of Jesus, there were still

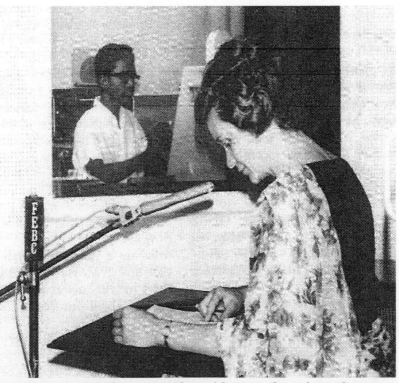

Radio programs require more than Alma at the microphone. From sound engineers to children listening to the radio, lots of people and prayer are involved.

battles to be won.

On my first trip to Calcutta to make thirteen programs, I had recorded only nine minutes when the main tube in the tape recorder blew out. It took several days for the engineer to comb Calcutta before he finally found the correct replacement.

Another time I arrived in Calcutta by train in the evening only to find the city paralyzed by a hartal, a complete strike in which all businesses and services are forced to shut down. I couldn't leave the railway station because of the strike and was forced to sleep under a whirling fan in the waiting room. The next morning I was hoarse. I sounded like the bear that went over the mountain.

In order to avoid the expensive time-consuming trip to Calcutta, we decided to try recording in a Finnish friend's home in Ghoom, just a few miles from us. Riitta Siikanen had a good quality dependable Uher tape recorder.

We waited until after the last Darjeeling train shrilled its way past the nearby crossing before we began. By then it was 8:30 p.m., and invariably Riitta's Tibetan apso dog, Kuso, would start snoring beneath the warm wood stove. Such sounds would never pass international broadcast standards for a program to be aired from a powerful 100,000 watt station in Manila, Philippines. Eventually I learned to take my dog-lover friend, Meridel Fowler, along. She would lie on her tummy on the floor directly in front of the stove, quietly entertaining Kuso, so there was no more snoring to interrupt our recording.

We draped blankets over and in front of Riitta's narrow, boxlike clothes closet in which I sat with the mike. I pulled a string when I was ready, and Riitta began the recording in the next room.

All too frequently just at recording time there were unexpected blackouts from a city power failure. Or the electricity fluctuated so much that we couldn't record. We were totally dependent on the Lord for His help.

After a few years we built our own studio in a small room in Mission House. Flattened egg cartons covered the walls to absorb sound. God provided the studio, equipment and operating expenses to produce and air the program month by month, all in answer to prayer.

Treasure Hunt continued for ten years, first beamed to Asia from Manila and later from the Seychelles Islands with even better reception results. We offered Gospels, booklets and bookmarks to those who wrote in. Feedback came from Thailand, Nepal, and all parts of India.

Youngsters of all ages, college students, parents and grandparents, teachers, and even doctors wrote. The letters were often full of surprises. They were addressed to Auntie, Anty, Unty, Anti and Madam.

Some letters read:

> *"As suggested by you, I have asked Jesus to be my friend and Savior."*

> *"I am a listener to your broadcast and every Saturday I give patient hearing about the stories you tell me about Jesus and His Daddy."*

> *"I want to be a follower of Jesus Christ. Also I want to be the sinner of Christ."* *(He must have understood that Jesus loves sinners!)*

> *"If a little 6-year-old will stand glued to the radio for fifteen minutes every Saturday to hear a voice she cannot see, it must be interesting."*

Treasure Hunt had directed a lot of children to the true treasure in Jesus. But children's radio programs in English were just the beginning. The Lord had much more planned for Nepali programs, because the Nepalis must hear about "Jesus and His Daddy" too, but that's another story.

I was nearly tripped up on the next recording adventure.

Nearly Tripped Up!

"Please supply thirteen more children's radio programs!" came the urgent request from the Far East Broadcasing Company. This message came before our own studio was completed in Darjeeling, so I had to go to Calcutta.

At the same time, word came that an American eye specialist was at a Santal Mission Hospital in Mohulpahari, Bihar, until March tenth. We had several contacts with a nearly blind Sherpa friend, Jayti. Doctors prescribed glasses, injections, and ointments, to no avail. We all wondered, "Is there hope? Could Jayti regain her sight?"

Her family decided to drive to see the specialist for a good diagnosis. I would go with them and take the train the rest of the way to Calcutta to record *Treasure Hunt*.

Early in the morning of the seventh we pulled away from Darjeeling, the land rover crammed full with blind Jayti, her husband, sister, mother, niece, an alternate driver, our NISS artist and me. After two hours of swinging back and forth lower and lower from one curve to another, we were down from the mountains in the grilling heat of the plains. All day long we drove past bleak mud huts along roads lined with mango and palm trees.

Four of our party were Buddhists, and two were Hindus. I asked Jayti what she had learned of Jesus.

"Nothing," she replied, starting a long conversation about Him.

We arrived at the Ganges River and drove onto the ferry just minutes before it pulled away from shore. Half an hour later as we disembarked, we were saying, "If we had been five minutes later, think how detained we would have been! That was the last ferry today! Now we are only three hours away from the hospital."

We entered the next village at dusk. As we rounded a bend, an old man suddenly stepped out in front of the land rover without looking or apparently hearing. The land rover gave two sickening bumps as it unavoidably hit him and drove over him. We jumped out to see what could be done. He was dead!

We wondered whose father, whose husband he was. None of us had ever been involved in someone's death before. Angry, curious, talkative people rapidly formed a huge throng seemingly from nowhere. We asked someone to call the police. But there were no telephones. The nearest police station was ten miles away. A man set off on a bicycle for the police. The husband, who had driven so carefully and blown the horn incessantly seemed too stunned to believe his eyes. Some of the *dhoti*-clad villagers ripped off his watch and dragged him away.

"They are killing him! They are killing him!" screamed Jayti's mother. Jayti's blind eyes looked up in terror. Her sister and mother sobbed hysterically. Jayti nearly fainted from shock. Our one canteen of drinking water and a light fan were hopelessly inadequate. As the crowd grew thicker, the air filled with suffocating dust.

"Father, I refuse Satan and all his power in the name of Jesus and through the blood of the Lamb. You protect us, dear Father. Your Word says You will." That was all I could do. I simply had to pray and rest in Him.

I opened the door and stood on the floor of the land rover so that I could see over the top of the car into a sea of faces on every side and asked for attention. In very broken Hindi I explained that we were so very sorry this accident had happened, that we had stopped to help, that these passengers were not Chinese – as some were accusing them of being—but Sherpas. India's Mt. Everest's hero, Tenzing, was also a Sherpa.

We were taking a blind wife to a doctor, and she heard only their voices. Would these people please help us by bringing water and staying back from the car? The folk were encouragingly responsive. Some brought tea in little clay cups, others brought water. But everywhere there were eyes, sad liquid eyes, enormous brown eyes, all staring, tense and immensely direct.

I had brought Hindi tracts along, *After Death, What?* Dare I give them out in such circumstances, in such a crowd? Would they antagonize even more? The Lord gently reminded me of His "Fear

Alma and blind Jayti, along with the whole traveling party, were going to the hospital and Alma was going further to make radio recordings in Calcutta.

not!" A few tracts quietly passed out through the window caused a virtual stampede for "handbills," for all the books and tracts I had with me.

Hour after hour crept by. At nine p.m. the police inspector arrived. At one a.m. he finished his measuring and inquiring. Jayti's husband, distraught and sobbing, was brought back by the police. Over and over again I assured our traveling companions that the Living God would answer prayer, would help us.

In the wee small hours we arrived at the police station to catch a three-hour "wink" on the floor under swarms of mosquitoes. The next day we were to go to the county seat and courthouse.

"Be sure you see the Lawyer Khasi Babu," the police said.

Heads turned when our party made its way by rickshaw to the local railway station that morning, since the land rover had to be left behind to be inspected. Such a party of police, Mongolian-looking hill people and a foreign lady dressed in a sari was a sight to behold!

We climbed up the steep rungs of the train steps. The train jerked unexpectedly. We were on our way. The police unlocked the handcuffs, and Jayti's husband sat on the floor, head on the seat. Could he be released on bail? How long would it take? How could I get Jayti to the specialist with thirty-six hours left to go? Thoughts tumbled in wild confusion. Her husband looked imploringly, "Do try to get me released, older sister!" I could only point him to the Living Father in heaven and remind him that I, too, was helpless without Him.

Four hours later our train arrived at the county seat, and our procession of rickshaws creaked from the railway station into the courthouse yard. A neatly dressed gentleman approached us. "May I help you?" he asked.

"Yes, could we please have some drinking water!" Introductions followed. This was Khasi Babu, whom the Lord had sent!

Within an unbelievably short time of three hours, Khasi Babu had the husband released on bail and the car released, pending a checkup by a certain mechanic fifty miles away. Our hearts were full of thanksgiving and praise.

Since the land rover could not be available in time for us to meet the specialist, we decided to follow Khasi Babu's travel suggestions. After another nearly sleepless night of dozing in chairs, we took a four a.m. bus to Murarai where we were to catch a six a.m. train.

I didn't see how we could possibly get the party of eight and large stuffy bedrolls of mattresses and pillows into an already overcrowded third-class compartment in the train. So we bought tickets for first class.

The train steamed into the station. We ran down the length of the train looking for a first-class compartment. Our coolie carrying bedding shoved his load into the train. I followed up the steps with bags, turned to help the others when the train started moving. It hadn't stopped for more than three minutes. There I was with half the luggage and all the rest of the party left behind on the platform. The conductor and two other men pulled hard at the chain, always part of Indian train equipment, that would stop the train in an emergency. I called back to Jayti that the train would stop in a minute. Her hand rested assuringly on her sister's shoulder. But the train didn't stop! It only gained speed as it carried me away from my party.

The next train in the same direction wouldn't leave until eight hours later – too late to reach the specialist. We had to make connections some other way. There were no jeeps to be rented, not even horse drawn carts. Helpful fellow travelers assured me that I could return back to the station if I caught another train at the next stop.

Ten minutes later the train creaked to a halt. I hurried across the tracks with a coolie in tow and got onto a train heading back to Murarai. What a relief to feel the train start back to my friends. Before it had come to a full stop at Murarai I had hailed a coolie to help carry the luggage. The train shuddered to a stop. I jumped off, looking eagerly for the others. They were nowhere to be seen!

When I asked the Station Master if he had seen a group of Nepalis, he replied, "Oh yes! How could anyone have missed them? They are outside the station."

Then I spotted Jayti's husband's orange shirt in a big bus just pulling away. My shout had never stopped a bus before, but it did that day! A relieved, happy reunion was punctuated with chuckles and sighs mixed with, "Thank YOU, Father, thank You!"

After one more change by bus we arrived at the hospital at Mohulpahari. Mrs. Bill Scott met me with "We've been looking for you, Alma. The eye specialist left four days early, the day before your telegram arrived!"

A very careful examination by the hospital doctors showed that Jayti's optic nerve was severely damaged and irreparable. Nothing could be done. We bathed, ate our second meal in three days, had other checkups and rested. Because of a Communist statewide strike in West Bengal, we were forced to wait in the adjoining state, Bihar. We sat on mats and talked about Jesus' being the best of all lawyers, the best of intermediaries for condemned men. We had learned a little of what it was to have Jesus plead our case for us.

Early in the morning we started for the railway station, Jayti's party to return to where the land rover had been kept, whereas I was to go on to Calcutta where I still had thirteen broadcasts to record.

We did not know that trains had been burned, stations left in shambles, and tracks torn up in that devastating strike. Jayti and her folk had to wait at the station the whole day while I caught the one and only train that could go to Burdwan, only half way to Calcutta. I sat alone in the train compartment there for eight uncertain hours as tracks were repaired and sad reports came in over the telegraph wires. The Lord's sustaining presence was very real.

Finally the Calcutta-bound train inched away from Burdwan station. Military police armed with guns and steel helmets guarded the train front and back. Four hours later we had covered the sixty miles to volatile Calcutta.

To my surprise, Calcutta's Howrah Station area was not choked by the usual mass of taxis, *tongas*, rickshaws, and pedestrians. A citywide strike had stopped everything. Businesses and services were shut down. Though it was only 9 p.m., there wasn't a soul on the street. Curfew was in order! I joined the stranded passengers cluttering the ladies' waiting room for the night.

The next morning big black crows announced the first faint streaks of light. I hailed a rickshaw and climbed in. The bell in the runner's hand sounded a dull clink, clink as he made his way to the mission guest house. I was so grateful to finally be ready to start the strenuous work of recording broadcasts. The enemy of our souls had certainly tried to hinder my coming, but he was defeated. Without even knowing my need, I was sure prayer partners had been praying! They had been praying for future believers they knew nothing about.

Chapter 10

God's Faithfulness

Better than Leopard Skins

Before the door opened to Nepal, "flat missionaries" were making their way over shaky bridges into that land. Bir Bahadur Rai was living in Dhankuta in eastern Nepal when someone handed him *The Way of Salvation* printed in Nepali. He read it avidly. Four years later someone gave him a Nepali Bible. That, too, he read eagerly.

For many years the law of Nepal required that if one caused someone else to convert from Hinduism to another religion, he would be imprisoned for six years. If one converted from Hinduism to another religion, he would be imprisoned for a year and lose all his inheritance. Despite all that, Bir Bahadur wrote his personal testimony for the *SANGATI* magazine in December 1961, one of the NISS Christian magazines in Nepali.

This is what he wrote:

"I went on reading the Bible, and in 1958 I accepted Christ as my Savior while I was in Okhaldunga through the verse in Matthew 10:28 which reads: 'Fear not them which kill the body, but are not able to kill the soul; rather fear him which is able to destroy both soul and body in hell.'

"I was a member of a family worshiping many kinds of idols. But the Lord Jesus gave me courage. I knew that only God can destroy my body and soul. Then why should I fear the idols? So, to really worship God in spirit and in truth, I became a part of Christ's body.

"For two years, I lived at Tansen, Palpa, West Nepal. In 1960 I had the opportunity to go to the Bible school at Mirik, in Darjeeling, a district of W. Bengal, India. There I studied for a year, during which time God offered me blessed fellowship with His children. I had applied to the Principal of the School to take me in as a student for two years, but that was not the will of God. And at present, I am experiencing

*His will by living in some kind of discipline in a place where
there are two hundred-forty persons. The place with this rule
of discipline in vogue is prison.*

*"This year (1960) God has in many ways blessed me
with the opportunity to experience His blessings. The
outward worldly man in me is being destroyed, but the inner
man in me is becoming new day by day.*

*"Many of my friends, on the spur of the moment for their
love for me, asked me why I was prepared to face such
tribulations. They suggested to me to leave my Lord and get
out of the fire. They asked me to deny my Lord.*

*"But I ignored their suggestions. 'Whoever shall deny
Me before men, him will I also deny before my Father who is
in heaven,' (Matt.10:33); 'He that rejects Me, rejects not
man, but God, who hath also given us His Holy Spirit'(1
Thess.4:8). These words were ever before me. And God in
His mercy gave me power to stand fast before the onslaught
of such temptations. God changed me. He made me fit and
able to suffer for His name's sake. Praise the Lord!"*

Nine Nepali believers were summoned to court, one by one, and
interrogated.

"What had the foreigners paid them to become Christians?" "How
had they been forced to change their religion?"

They had answered without fear:

*"No, we were not bribed. No, we were not forced by any-
one or by any means. We have personally believed upon
Jesus Christ, and determined to follow Him, no matter what
the cost."*

The pastor who had baptized them was sent to prison for six years
along with the new believers. In prison, there was great deprivation of
mind, soul, and body for the ten Christians. The prison was filthy.
There were endless opportunities for the new prisoners to show
kindness and practical opportunities of love. They taught their fellow
prisoners about sanitation and the basics of reading, writing and
arithmetic. But best of all, they shared their own testimonies.

One evening over a year later, we heard a faint tap at our door.
When we opened the door, there were three believers who had recently

been released from prison. Now they were on their way to Darjeeling Hills Bible School. We were honored and privileged to have them make their home with us for several weeks.

Humbly they shared their prison experiences. How gratefully they described their release. Dal Bahadur told how their Bibles were taken away from them but finally returned. After this they hid them. At night when everyone else was sleeping, they took them out and read by candlelight.

Bir Bahadur took out his Bible and I gasped with surprise. Twelve years earlier, I had bought a plastic raincoat with an imitation leopard skin design. In the heavy monsoon rains, I had completely worn it out. I gave it to the Bible school men to use however they wished. They had cut it in lengths for covering and protecting their books. It is very common for Nepalis to cover school books with pages of magazines. Bir had covered his Bible with the plastic leopard skin and it had been with him all through prison. But more than seeing that old plastic was the joy of seeing how those dear brothers and sisters had studied and fed on the Word of God!

Little did Bir Bahadur and his fellow prisoners know that in 1990 Nepal's constitution would be changed to nominally provide religious freedom.

"Every person shall have the freedom to profess and practice his own religion as coming down to him from perennial past with due regard to the traditional practices. . . Every religious community shall have the right to maintain its independent existence, and for the purpose to manage and protect its religious sites and trusts."[32]

The constitution would still prohibit conversion: "Provided that no person shall be entitled to convert another person from one religion to another."

Yet, because of the 1990 democracy movement, that provision would not be actively enforced. The result has been phenomenal growth of the church. In 2006, a newly restored Parliament would declare Nepal no longer a Hindu Kingdom, but a secular state. A Constitutional Convention is being called to rewrite the nation's constitution.

Our own son Paul would forge a bond that would reach into far

---

[32] Constitution, Kingdom of Nepal, Kathmandu: Ministry of Law & Justice, His Majesty's Government, Nepal, 2047 (1990 AD).

western Nepal where he would experience first hand the impact of Nepal's persecution of Christians.

Strong Bonds Forged

Roy and I had accompanied seventeen-year-old David to Calcutta and seen him fly off into a dazzling sunrise on his way to a new life in America. He had left home and was changing life in the East to life in the West, and from British schooling to American. Chemistry Professor Bob Olson and his family had offered him a home away from home. So he chose to attend Pacific Lutheran University to study Chemistry and Physics. Now our family was down to five.

But our house rang with laughter and fun. San Ruohoniemi worked as hospital administrator for the UMN hospital in Kathmandu. The Ruohoniemi family of eight had come to stay two weeks with us. It was January and cold in Darjeeling. Roy and San worked long hours thrashing out a constitution for a new publishing society, *Nepali Isai Sahitya Sangha*, Nepali Christian Literature Society, (NISS). This combined the printing press and the publishing all under one roof. The six Ruohoniemi children, four girls and two boys, and our three sons played games by the hour in our one heated room in the house.

When wash day came, we sent all the young people on a day's excursion to Ghoom. It would take three days to dry the clothes outdoors hanging under the eaves, but only one day if we hung them on ropes stretched across the heated dining/living room. So we packed lunches and sent the youngsters hiking.

Joyce Ruohoniemi and I spent time in the kitchen, preparing meals for thirteen. We were chopping vegetables and stirring soup one day when Joyce and I spoke almost simultaneously, "Paul and Becky are meant for each other!" We didn't dare breathe a word but we knew. Was that the Lord's direction? Or were mothers only dreaming?

The next month our family drove by jeep to Nepal. Road repairs were being done on the main road to Kathmandu, so for a stretch we had to drive along the river bed and crisscross the river eight times. The water reached above the hub caps. When brake linings get wet they get slippery and simply don't work.

Just as we came out of the river onto the narrow highway, a bus came barreling down the road toward us. We met it just at a point where a huge boulder had rolled onto our side of the highway. We had no brakes. A fence and a sharp drop were on our side of the road. But we had God's angelic protection and miraculously got by with only a scratch.

Space scientists, astronomers, and advisors to NASA, Tuscon-based Drs. Aden and Marge Meinel, met us in Kathmandu. We insisted they see beautiful Pokhara. We boarded an old DC-3 freight plane, crawling over huge piles of fruit saplings and fertilizer tied down in the middle of the plane. We strapped ourselves into our seats parallel with the windows. Aden and Marge sat across from Roy and me. We lifted our hands up committing our trip to the Lord.

Moments after the plane took off, we heard a loud noise. Aden saw something grey fly past his window. Looking out the windows over our shoulders, we realized we were not gaining altitude but were rapidly circling down. Suddenly we were back on the runway. The pilot and co-pilot came out of the cockpit shaking glass out of their shirts. We had hit a flock of birds that completely shattered half of the windshield. God had again spared us.

After a four-hour wait we boarded another DC-3 and finally were able to show our dear friends the majesty of the Annapurna range from beautiful Pokhara.

In Pokhara we also introduced them to the Green Pastures Leprosarium. There illiterates were being taught to read and many of our NISS books were being enjoyed. The Shining Hospital that Pat and Hilda had begun, as well as the Gandaki Boarding School, also made good use of that Christian literature.

It is hard to put into words the friendships that missionaries develop. Relationships with others are not without challenges, but on the mission field, we formed strong bonds with many co-workers that helped us through turbulent times.

Rescued Again

Four American high school students had come from Chicago during summer holidays to experience school life in an English-medium school in India. They were sitting in on classes with our boys at Mt. Hermon School in Darjeeling. They soon found that the spelling was different, the pronunciation was different, the food was different, everything was different.

They knew we were leaving shortly on furlough. "Could you please take us to a game reserve to see rhinos?" they begged. It would be a good outing for our boys before we had to leave Paul behind to finish high school. We agreed to take them.

After a six-hour jeep ride and a short sleep, we climbed up on two elephants: Paul, Ken, Karl and I on one elephant, the four from Chicago on the other. Then we were off to see rhinos. We plodded through one area of jungle to a usual rhino watering spot, but there was nothing to see; so we headed for the river. We had driven through the same river in January, but now it was a rushing torrent swollen by monsoon rains.

I thought, "Not across that!"

Our *mahout* said, "We'll cross it!" and headed right for a very swift part. Our elephant crossed first, inch by inch, with his rear to the current. For many minutes we simply didn't make any visible progress. There was swirling, rushing water all around us, right up to our elephant's mouth. It seemed ages before we got across.

Just as we arrived at the farther shore, Ken cried out "Oh no!"

We turned and saw that fifteen-year-old Joan had slipped off her elephant and was barely hanging on to the iron frame of the saddle. Only her head and shoulders were visible. The current had pulled her feet under the elephant. We prayed, "Jesus, save her!" We watched breathlessly as the mahout and seventeen-year-old Steve Townley slowly tugged her up by one arm. Gradually they pulled her up onto the saddle. What a relief to see her safely back on the elephant!

On our return across the river, we switched partners. Joan sat in front of me with both of her feet behind the mahout and my arms around her waist so she wouldn't fall off. We made it safely across.

We never did see the rhinos, but our praises and thanksgivings to the Lord were profuse for days afterward. He had proved His faithfulness to us again. I wonder how many angels He sent to be with us on that trip.

Another person who would experience God's faithfulness had an important position in India's Parliament.

From Parliament to Prayer

"You're short!" commented the visitor to plucky Arun.

"That's obvious!" was her candid reply. She might have been a "half-pint" in physical size, but she was tall in spirit.

We had recently moved back to Darjeeling from Mirik when I met Arun on the street one day.

"Alma, if you would just wear a sari, your legs wouldn't show!" she declared very matter-of-factly. I took this social correction seriously from an older Nepali sister, got out a pale lavender cotton sari, and began to wear it. The first day I walked to the vegetable market in a plain sari, I longed for the street manholes to open up so I could disappear. But the Lord helped me overcome pride, and wearing a sari became a habit for twenty years to follow.

This feisty little lady was the granddaughter of the famed Ganga Prasad Pradhan, who was one of the first Nepali Hindus in Darjeeling District to be converted. "He was born July 4, 1851, in Tamel Kot, Kathmandu...He grew up as an illiterate young Newar. As a young

Prayer partners Theodore and Arun Manaen flank Roy and Alma.

man he worked tilling his father's fields and later as a coolie on a tea plantation near Darjeeling. No one would have suspected that he would one day be the first ordained Nepali pastor, translator of the Nepali Bible, pioneer in Nepali literature and owner of the first Nepali press."[33] He was known for his eloquence in preaching and faithfulness to the Lord.

Arun came often to our home to intercede for her husband, Theodore Manaen. Theodore had been a classmate of Shilling's when the two attended the Turnbull Boys' High School in Darjeeling, which was just down the hill from the Scots Mission House. After difficulties finding just the right job, Theodore's dad became the manager of Mt. Hermon School, a position he held for thirty years.

When WMPL pioneer in Nepali work, Jonathan Lindell, first visited Darjeeling, he and Theodore spent many happy hours together. They translated the Gospel of Mark into simple Nepali. They hiked around Darjeeling District for three weeks.

After his studies at Scottish College in Calcutta, Theodore had been asked to teach political science and history in the Nepali Girls' School. Arun was teaching Nepali in the same school. They were married soon after they began teaching there. The longer he taught political science, the more he wanted to enter that field. He saw it as an opportunity to serve the Nepalis, not as an opportunity for financial gain. Theodore's "gift of gab" opened doors for favor in politics. Running for the Congress Party, he lost the election in the West Bengal Assembly in 1952, but he won a seat in India's National Parliament in 1957 and again in 1962. Thus he was a Member of the Parliament in India's Lok Sabha (similar to the House of Commons) for ten years. He was elected General Secretary of the Indian National Congress party from 1964 to 1967. During his tenure he served in that high position under Prime Ministers, Pandit Jawaharlal Nehru, Lal Bahadur Shastri and Indira Gandhi.

During this time, Arun would often pop-in, and ask for prayer for Theodore. In 1967 he lost the election by 300 votes but got 30,000 votes in another county. Later Theodore said, "I don't know why I wanted to leave politics. It just seemed empty."

He gave us a glimpse into politics when we asked him, "What was

---

[33] Cindy Perry, *A Biographical History of the Church in Nepal*, Nepal Church History Project, Kathmandu, p. 32, 1993.

the most difficult thing in your life at the 'top' of the country?"

"Cliques and compromise!" came the straightforward reply.

Ultimately, he closed the door to politics, and returned to Darjeeling. He began to pray and earnestly read the Bible. He encouraged some of the men of the local Nepali church to pray together and to seek God's plan in His Word.

One day he and Roy stood at the Mission Compound gate. Of his earlier life Theodore said, "All my beautiful young years I have given to the devil." To that Roy replied, "God will restore the years that the locust has eaten."[34]

In 1968, Mr. Paul Lindell, director of World Mission Prayer League, wrote to Roy. He asked if we as a mission should invite Theodore and Arun to join the fellowship of the Prayer League as an Associate Director in the home office in Minneapolis. Roy discussed it with Theodore. Ten months later Theodore and Arun felt it was right to join WMPL, so they accepted. There was an open door before them. Paul Lindell wrote them, "We can't promise you salary and goods, but we can set two more plates here on the table and we will pray that the Lord would supply the bread."

They finally arrived in Minneapolis in October, 1972, where they served for the next fifteen years. Later they were reassigned to India. They taught for two years at the Darjeeling Hills Bible School. Then Theodore helped establish a congregation in Siliguri.

When the Manaens were first introduced in Minneapolis, the WMPL staff were asked to tell where they were from. Arun responded, "I am from India, stopping in Minneapolis, going to heaven."

In 2000 she was back in Minneapolis where she died of an enlarged heart. She is now beholding our lovely Lord. God answered prayer. I am sure she stands tall in heaven.

Arun's prayers helped move Theodore from Parliament to preaching. God answered more prayers in amazing ways.

Three Near Tragedies

As we left for furlough in July 1968, Paul bade us a brave "goodbye." He would continue on in Darjeeling for four and a half months to complete his high school work, never anticipating he would

---

[34] Joel 2:25, KJV

experience a disaster.

When we reached Copenhagen en route to America, we were shocked to receive a cable from India. L.B. Rai, Roy's right-hand man in the JJP office, had been in a bad jeep accident and was hospitalized with a fractured pelvis and arm. This was a real blow to the work. His arm was eventually operated on one and a half months after the accident. Our good friend and former editor, Dinesh Khaling, came to the rescue in the office, but we were reminded again that we were in a spiritual battle. We knew that Jesus is Lord!

Folk had raised one eyebrow asking if it wasn't risky and "uncertain" to live as we did, trusting God for all things. Our plans may have looked uncertain, but God's plans and provision were certain and we delighted to rest in Him.

Flying over the Atlantic, Roy studied articles on buying second-hand cars. A family of five needed wheels to get around in America.

After arriving in New York, we stayed with Roy's brother Erling. The purchase of a necessary second-hand car came up as we ate breakfast.

Erling said, "I think we'll sell the Pontiac." He was referring to the '65 Pontiac Catalina station wagon. Roy hardly dared to ask the price, knowing its value was double what we had saved for a car. I nearly choked on my bacon when Erling added, "I think we'll sell it for $800." He didn't know that we had exactly $800 allocated for a car. And at that time neither Erling nor we knew why we would need a station wagon rather than an ordinary four-passenger car, but our Heavenly Father knew.

We had expected to stay in Minneapolis on our furlough. When we wired our son David in Tacoma, Washington, asking if he would like to transfer to the University of Minnesota in Minneapolis, he wired back, "I have found a house for you. Shall I rent it?"

We agreed and proceeded to Tacoma. There David had not only found a house but had it fully furnished, right down to dishes and pots and pans.

Paul had written from Mount Herman School in Darjeeling that he would soon be visiting the Bergs, WMPL missionaires, in Mirik. A short while later, October sixth, we read in the newspaper that Darjeeling, Ghoom, and Kurseong were in "near ruins," and that 30,000 were dead in Mirik. Twenty-six inches of continous rain came down in sixty hours, starting dreadful landslides all over Darjeeling

District. Whole villages, where we had recently sold Gospels and shared the good news of a living Savior, were washed away or buried in mud.

All communications were cut. It was impossible to phone or telegraph Darjeeling. Only after sixteen long days did we learn of Paul's safety. His plans had changed. He had not gone to Mirik, but had remained in Darjeeling. The news report of 30,000 dead in Mirik was completely wrong.

Paul wrote that Mount Hermon School was using its swimming pool as an emergency water supply. They had no hot water to wash with for a month. The students helped carry blankets to the homeless in the Mount Hermon area.

One pitch-black night, Paul and another student were crossing a hillside to help some faculty members. His friend, carrying their only flashlight, was ahead of Paul. Paul stopped to clear the path of some bushes. Suddenly, a land slide came down right in front of him, separating him from his friend carrying the flashlight. Had Paul not stopped to clear the path, he would have been swept down the mountain in the dark. Father God still had a future for Paul.

Letters finally began to flow out of Darjeeling from many friends. All reflected similar horrors. Folk were still in a daze. One of our printers lost his parents and three sisters when their home was buried in mud. Jonathan Thapa, our press manager, wrote, "Many people were killed, buried, or swept away. All the hills around Darjeeling look like a great angry bear had clawed the hill. Darjeeling stinks of mud and misery. We need your prayers more than ever."

Our Nepali colleagues worked hard at rescue and relief work. They printed a timely folder comforting people, encouraging them to take necessary health precautions, and pointing them to the way of salvation.

We spent a school year in Tacoma, Washington. Paul returned from India and enrolled in Bible school.

Shortly before we were to return to India, we were at a Bible camp in Saskatchewan. It was time for afternoon sports and a baseball game. Roy hit the first pitch and slid into third base. On that slide, he fractured and dislocated his hip. When nearby doctors looked at his x-ray, they insisted such a complicated break necessitated his being airlifted to the University Hospital in Saskatoon to have it properly taken care of. After surgery he was put in a long cast from his waist to his toes. He watched America's first moon-landing from his hospital bed.

When he was finally ready to travel, we understood better why our Father God had provided a station wagon instead of an ordinary sedan. We made a bed in the back of our station wagon and Roy rode safely back to Tacoma. There our dear friends, Ken and Stella Jacobs, gave us their master bedroom for Roy to recuperate in.

Ken and Karl, fifteen and fourteen, had to return to India by themselves to complete the school year at Mt. Hermon.

The mercies of the Lord were new every morning! We received them! We thanked the Lord for them!

We would soon be receiving still more mercies when we moved into Nepal, finally walking through that door that had opened to others twenty years before.

Chapter 11

Nepalis Leading

Ministry Extended

1972 was a historic year for Jiwan Jyoti Prakashan (Light of Life Publishers) and our family.

We had been sitting on Nepal's doorstep for twenty years watching the door begin to open. In 1970, we felt it was time for us to walk through that door into Kathmandu itself. We wanted to extend the literature ministry into Nepal through Himalaya Prakashan, Himalayan Publishers, (HP) to do graphic printing and publishing inside Nepal. By November 1970, Roy had registered Himalaya Prakashan in Nepal.

Roy applied for the import permits to bring in the graphics and phototypesetting equipment. His Majesty's Government gave Roy all kinds of verbal assurances of approval. We moved into Kathmandu in January 1971.

A Danish printing consultant and a Swedish printing expert offered to help design the project. Our California friend, Mr. Fred Nielson, shipped a press to Calcutta, while we applied for import licenses. Roy obtained a major grant from a donor agency in Germany which provided ample funds for the proposed printing, publishing and sales program. This would train nationals in the necessary technical and business skills to carry it on.

Meanwhile, Roy's able assistant in Darjeeling, Adon Rongong, moved to Nepal. With Roy's help, he began a flourishing book store in the center of Patan, a city next to Kathmandu. Since then, Adon and his wife Manu have blessed Nepal from one end to the other, both in their witness through Campus Crusade for Christ, and also through women's prayer groups organized by Manu.

When Roy and I moved into Nepal, Dibya Khaling also moved to Kathmandu. Dibya was gifted in composing, playing, and singing to the heart of the Nepalis. We turned our cookhouse into a recording studio. Many Nepali programs for the Far East Broadcasting Company were produced there to be beamed from Manila or the Seychelles

Islands back to Nepal.

At the same time, Bible translation was going on at two levels. A simple version was being prepared for those who had just started reading. The second common language version was being prepared, similar to *Today's English Version*. All who could read the JJP Bible stories and selections would soon be able to read God's Word.

K.P. Bhattarai was the key Nepali translator for these versions. Some friends with the Summer Institute of Linguistics also assisted Roy and K.P. It was a momentous day when the Common Language Version was finally printed, after years of laborious work. But then two evangelical "brothers" in Kathmandu, not Nepalis, decided it wasn't fit to read because the Nepali translation said, "Jesus turned the water into wine." They insisted "wine" should have been translated as non-

Popular Nepali composer and singer Dibya Khaling with soul-winner and leader Adon Rongong in Patan, Nepal.

alcoholic "grape juice." So they gathered as many of copies of the Common Language Version as they could and burned them right in Kathmandu. Translator heartaches! The Lord taught us we must forgive.

I remember so well just where I was standing in our kitchen one day when the Lord spoke clearly to me through Matthew 4:10, "Worship the Lord your God and serve Him." Worship came first, then service. I had them back to front. I had been serving, but worshiping very little. When I asked the Lord's forgiveness, He gave me great joy in putting worship first.

That resulted in our having a "Praise and Worship" gathering in our home every Thursday evening. Nationals as well as internationals came to praise and worship. It was a blessed time.

While on a previous trip to the States, we had met a Mrs. Hintz who asked us to contact her son, Fred, working in Nepal with the Peace Corps. We sent him a note and he came for tea the same day that Ruth Heflin, well-known Pentacostal missionary, was visiting us. Ruth had already made inroads witnessing to the royal family of Nepal. It was the cook's day off, so I apologetically excused myself to prepare supper. Ruth and Fred continued talking in the living room. Within an hour, Fred had surrendered his heart to Jesus as well as received the baptism of the Holy Spirit. He was a changed person, giving up drinking, smoking and gambling.

Later Fred completed his work out in the hinterland and moved to Kathmandu to live in our little "Prophet's Chamber" on the flat roof of our home, where he gave himself to studying the word of God. His genuine witness to the many foreign hippies who came to Kathmandu was not to be forgotten. Nor was his help with the Nepal Leprosy Trust, where he helped many former leprosy patients be rehabilitated on the warm lowlands of Nepal. Eventually Fred went back to the States to care for his mother, who was dying of cancer.

Our friends working in western Nepal continued to write that they just could not keep up with the demand for Christian literature and the thirst to hear the word of God.

Then in May 1972 came the bombshell that His Majesty's Government had refused to grant the import permits for all the equipment for Himalayan Publishing that had been sitting on the docks in Calcutta. A company with no equipment was effectively defunct.

Roy began to sell off the equipment, and return the grants. While officially liquidating the company, he made the most of the opportunity to work on Bible translation and make Nepali radio programs.

Wind over the Mountains

In September, 1974, the Inspector General of Police routinely stamped Roy's passport with approval for another six months' stay in Nepal. A few days later Roy was called to the Immigration Office. His visa was cancelled without any explanation and he was ordered to leave. After some petitioning, the Home Minister kindly granted Roy ten days to wind up his affairs!

Security arrangements for the coming coronation of Prince Birendra resulted in many foreigners being evicted. Hippies by the truckload were unceremoniously dropped off at the Indian border. Not only Roy, but all the Summer Institute of Linguistics translators, Prince Basundra's Venezuelan cook, and anyone else that was not under a big government-sponsored "umbrella" were forced to leave. (On later reflection, the fact we had rented a house next to a large foreign embassy was not helpful either.)

Roy proceeded to a Bible translators conference in Rajpur, India, where he had already been scheduled to speak. Later he was able to come back to Nepal on a brief tourist visa to help transfer all our work into the hands of Nepalis. This was our goal in the first place. God's timing was so different from ours, but we were learning.

My visa was good for another three months without any objections. Our son Paul had come on a tourist visa to be with us for the same length of time to help with Bible translation. During those next months, we helped with a big Vacation Bible School for more than two-hundred children, and a very anointed conference for Christian Nepalis. Before we left Nepal, Mary Verghese, a South-Indian missionary working in Nepal, had a vision of our teaching Asian children. "But they are not Nepalis," she added.

The previous year Alan Vincent had come to Kathmandu for special meetings and had given this encouraging prophecy:

> As the wind cannot be shut up or contained, so the wind of God cannot be shut up or contained. He shall blow as He will and none shall hinder.
> And I say unto you, saith the Lord, to **prophesy** to that

wind, that the wind may come upon you and cause you to come together as a body. Prophesy to the wind, and the wind shall come.

*And I say unto you, **pray** unto the wind, and the wind shall come.*

*And I say unto you, **sing** unto the wind and the wind shall come. And He shall breathe upon the bones and give them life, and He shall compact them together.*

And as you prophesy, and as you pray, and as you sing, you will see these things come to pass.

And I, the Lord, in response to your praying and prophesying, will cause that body to be formed. And I will give the body flesh and muscle, and I shall make that body strong in the Lord and in the power of His might, and it shall stand upon its feet and it shall be strong and do exploits. And the wind of God shall blow right to the four corners of this land, down every valley, across every mountain, in the dense, deep places, the wind shall blow, and everywhere it blows, it shall bring life and liberty.

Prepare yourselves for this day, the day of My power, saith the Lord, is almost upon you. Prepare yourselves for that day and make ready that you are not taken by surprise.

Rejoice, for that day of the visitation of God is upon you. It is not because of your holiness or because of your strength, says the Lord, but it is because of My mercy and My grace. Because I shall get for Myself a people out of these hills also, saith the Lord.

So call upon the Wind, and it shall blow, to the glory of My name.

The test of a true prophetic word is in its coming to pass. It may take years to happen, but at this writing, the church in Nepal is growing numerically and spiritually, despite Maoist insurgents' deadly attacks.

Though Roy's efforts to start Himali Prakashan were blocked, Adon's book store in Patan, continued to grow. He later moved it into Kathmandu and renamed it Ekta Books (meaning Oneness or Unity in Nepali). Adon then leveraged his printing and publishing training under Roy at JJP in Darjeeling, and launched into publishing books in Nepal.

Ekta Books has since become a major publishing and distribution house for educational and general books. When Adon had to leave Nepal, he returned to Siliguri and set up the Indian arm of Ekta Books.[35] Between the Nepali and Indian branches, Ekta Books now employs over one thousand people. The mustard seed of a tiny bookstore planted in Kathmandu has now become a major publishing tree.

Bible correspondence courses are another way literature has influenced Nepal. Hastaman Rai, one of the Bible school graduates, headed up one of the first Nepali Bible correspondence courses. At least three organizations are now providing Bible correspondence courses in Nepal. These grew rapidly in the 1990's. By 2004, one ministry distributed course materials to about 300,000 students.

A number of groups have been working to distribute literature in Nepal and to Nepalis internationally. One of Roy's NISS colleagues went on to head up a major literature outreach program in Nepal that has been working to systematically reach every village. Those involved report numerous testimonies of how people's lives and homes were changed by the truth and light of the Gospel through the literature they read.

After Roy left Nepal, the Lord gave him an encouraging word from Jeremiah 24:4-6: "Like these good figs, I regard as good the exiles from Judah, whom I sent away from this place in the land of the Babylonians. My eyes will watch over them for their good, and I will bring them back to this land. I will build them up and not tear them down, I will plant them and not uproot them."

Two months later our very dear Nepali pastor, Robert Karthak, wrote us an encouraging letter to share a promise the Lord had given him regarding our return to Nepal. It was the identical verse. "Thank You, Father!"

Over the years, we returned to Nepal several times. We had the privilege of speaking at Christian conferences. As often as we could, we visited Paul's family during the thirteen years they served in Nepal.

However, I certainly didn't feel like a "good fig" the day I rode the pony express!

---

[35] Ekta Books Distributors Pvt. Ltd. Kathmandu & Ekta Book House Pvt. Ltd., Siliguri WB India. http://www.ektabooks.com

Pony Express

Our special friend, Betty Bailey, who had founded Green Pastures Leprosarium along with Eileen Lodge, lived with a medical team in Ghorahi, in the far western region of Nepal. Twice a week, a Royal Nepal Airlines plane flew from Kathmandu to Tulsipur airport, seventeen miles from Ghorahi. Every week I dispatched a big, gray canvas bag containing mail, tinned butter and cheese to Betty. She and her friends were ever grateful for the mainstay of these goodies I sent out to go with her homemade brown bread.

They knew we were soon leaving Nepal. "You must come visit us before you leave," Betty wrote. Roy gave me the "go ahead" for a quick trip to Ghorahi, after a hectic time of packing up our household.

Dressed in my usual cotton sari, I tucked my Bible, toothbrush, flashlight and a change of clothes into a shoulder bag. I took the Ghorahi mailbag and started off for Kathmandu airport to fly to Tulsipur on the Wednesday flight.

After an hour and a half in the air, the sixteen-seat plane bumped down onto a large grassy field. Betty's errand man met me, putting his hands together in respectful Nepali greeting. He slung the bag onto his shoulder and took the mailbag in his hand; I carried some bacon and cheese and we were off. His bare feet left little puffs of dust behind as he walked ahead of me. I hurried to keep up.

We hopscotched precariously from one rock to another to cross the river. Then we pushed on, hiking mile after mile down the broad flat valley. The sun had already slipped behind the encircling mountains as we reached Ghorahi. The locals were lighting their kerosene lamps and the air was filled with smoke from cooking fires.

I was scheduled to fly back a week later. "It'll take a week to get my sore muscles back to normal," I thought.

It was a joy to see how the medical team was treating the patients. The unity and commitment among the nationals and internationals was obvious.

Saturday evening, Peter Bisset, a member of the medical team, came in for supper with the news, "Alma, a government minister has booked the whole plane to Kathmandu next Wednesday. You'll have to go back on tomorrow morning's plane." There were only two flights a week. My visa to Nepal expired the next week, so there was no postponing my departure. "I've made arrangements with a man who has a horse to take you to the airport," Peter added.

A horse! I hadn't ridden a horse in years!

I got up at four-thirty a.m. Betty brought me a cup of tea and crackers. We waited patiently for Peter—and then impatiently. I absolutely had to catch that plane. Finally Peter arrived at five-thirty. He had been so blessed in his early morning quiet time reading his Bible, he had forgotten what time it was!

We hurried down the cobblestone street to where Peter had scheduled the horse. Peter called to the owner. We heard a muffled cough, and then the vertical wooden boards forming the front wall of a shop began to move. Slowly the man came out, pushing more vertical slats aside to make room for the pony-sized horse to enter the street.

I was aghast! The horse was skin and bones. Its hip bones protruded like misplaced joints.

The man must have sensed my dismay.

"Don't worry, Memsahib!" he said as he dove back into the shop. Moments later he came out with gunnysacks filled with straw. He strapped these onto the horse, changing the shape of the animal completely.

How in the world was I to get on that "fat" creature wearing a floor-length sari?

The man led the horse to a ditch below the street level and indicated I should slide right on. Somehow I managed. Now my feet stuck out on either side of the horse like oars on a rowboat.

Amid muffled giggles, Betty, Peter and the others bade me farewell and we were off. The owner used a whip on the poor horse. "*Hut, hut, chull, chull*"[36] he coaxed the animal along. I prayed fervently that this low-speed horse would shift into high speed. It trotted for a short while and then continued its plodding pace.

A few miles out of Ghorahi, the early morning rays fell on a military contingent out for their morning exercise on the same road we were on. We dared not slow down to stay behind them. I had to catch that plane! The horse could not go much faster than the soldiers were marching. And there I was, right smack in the middle of the morning maneuvers.

"It's a nice day!" I said in Nepali, trying to break the embarrassment.

Each soldier looked straight ahead and spoke nary a word.

---

[36] Let's go. Let's go.

"It looks like it will be a nice warm day today, doesn't it?"

Every eye kept straight ahead. Finally the sergeant in charge called the troops to halt, and we trotted on.

At one point the owner suddenly said, "Hold on in front, and hold on in back!"

I grabbed the gunnysacks in front and in back just as the horse slid down into a deep ditch. As it climbed out on the opposite side, I looked back to see two skid tracks down the side of the bank.

Then we rode through the river. As we climbed out, I realized we were almost at the airfield. I begged the owner to lead the horse to a sloping bank so I could get off before I had to climb off in front of everyone at the airfield.

I managed to get my left foot down, but I was so stiff I could do nothing but waddle like a duck to get the right foot down. I could see out of the corner of my eye that the owner was highly amused.

Gradually I struggled up to the airfield. There I was ordered by a soldier posted at the gate "You can't enter now. There's a plane coming!"

"I know. I'm getting on it!"

"But you can't go!"

"But I must!"

Finally the guard acquiesced and let me, the horse, and the owner all cross, just a minute before the plane landed!

I quickly paid and thanked the owner. After my luggage and I were weighed, I climbed up the narrow steps to the plane whispering, "Thank You, Father, for traveling mercies on the pony express!"

Though I had ridden a pony through soldiers on maneuvers, I never expected that we would be assigned to a miliary area near the rear guard.

Chapter 12

Multiple Doors Open

By the Rear Guard

After we left Nepal, we prayed much for God's direction. WMPL wanted us to work among the Bengalis in Bangladesh. We took a course in Islam and began studying Bengali, but our hearts were still with the Nepalis.

So when Roy shared with our mission his vision of working among the ten thousand Nepali Gurkhas stationed in Hong Kong, our Director and the Mission Council immediately felt it was the right place for us to go. It became our new assignment from the Lord! Go to Hong Kong and minister to the Nepalis there.

Hong Kong! It was only 404 square miles, but it was the bargain basement of Asia, and the crossroad of East and West.

When the British ruled India in the 1800's they tried to conquer Nepal but were repulsed. The Nepalis are renowned as some of the fiercest hand-to-hand fighters in the world. These Nepalis soldiers are called Gurkhas. So the British turned around and hired Gurkhas to work in their army. They very successfully fought and defeated the Communist guerilla movement in Malaysia. Now 6,000 Gurkhas with 4,000 family members were working for the British Army in Hong Kong, at that time a British Crown Colony, to keep the peace and patrol the border with China.

Being a Gurkha was one of the most prized job opportunities for a Nepali. A Gurkha earned a high salary by Asian standards, had the opportunity to travel and learn English, and at the age of thirty-five or forty be retired with a lifetime pension. Gurkhas enjoyed respect and prestige in their villages when they returned. Many of these men have become effective witnesses for the Gospel.

On our arrival in Hong Kong we found a "leave flat" available right in the heart of Kowloon Tong. The owners would be away from Hong Kong in cool England for six weeks of summer. That would give us time to find a more permanent location.

Multiple Doors Open

We had been given the names and addresses of several Christian Gurkhas, so we invited them for Sunday afternoon fellowship.

How we rejoiced to find kindred spirits speaking Nepali right in the heart of Chinese Hong Kong. We were delighted to find them. They were happy to find us.

Kowloon Tong lay directly underneath the path of incoming international planes landing at Kai Tak Airport. The roar of the engines completely drowned out our singing and speaking. One Sunday afternoon we paused twenty-seven times during the fellowship time. The airport has since been changed to a nearby island.

Where should we locate? Seven Gurkha camps were scattered mainly in the New Territories, the northern part of Hong Kong.

A Norwegian friend telephoned saying, "There is a place for rent in Fanling advertised in the newspaper. I've only seen the beautiful garden. I'll ask my husband Bo to take you out to see it."

Bo drove us the hour's ride to Fanling. We turned off Jockey Club Road, down through tall palm trees, to a picture-book Chinese garden and house, hidden behind huge trees.

This was Sui Pak Yuen! White swans floated in a comma-shaped pond. A scarlet red teahouse and bridge curved over the water. More than a thousand bonsai plants lined the walks of this mini-park. The ninety-three-year-old owner was known for having the most beautifully groomed garden in all of the New Territories.

The available upstairs apartment and large verandah overlooking the garden was as beautiful as the layout below. The rent was US$350 per month. Could we afford that?

More important, was this where Father God wanted us to be?

We prayed, "Show us, Father, your mind and heart regarding where we should be."

I felt impressed to read Numbers 10:25 (Amplified): "Then the standard of the camp of the sons of Dan, which was the rear guard of all the camps, set forward according to their companies."

I was puzzled over the reference to the camp and the rear guard. We waited for the Gurkhas to come the following Sunday.

"We looked at a possible place to rent in Fanling," I said, explaining the location and our asking the Lord for direction. When I read out the verse the Lord gave us, the men were excited.

"My, my, older sister, don't you know? Almost directly across from Sui Pak Yuen is Pol-Mil, the rear guard of all the camps. Pol-Mil stands for Police-Military base, and every Gurkha in Hong Kong knows where Pol-Mil is!"

It turned out to be an ideal location. Throughout the ensuing five years, if we met a new Gurkha acquaintance and wanted to invite him to our home, we simply asked, "Do you know where Pol Mil is?"

"Yes, of course!"

"We live across the road from there behind the tall trees."

The official position of the British Army was to prevent any attempt to "proselytize" the Gurkhas. In 1947 an agreement was made between the governments of Nepal, India and the United Kingdom, which strongly opposed conversions to Christianity among the Gurkhas. This was done at a time when there were no known Nepali Christians inside Nepal. Despite all that, there were Christian believers among the soldiers. Some had become believers while on duty in England, and some of our closest friends and prayer partners in Hong Kong were British officers and their families.

Previously, if Christian Gurkhas tried to meet in public places or churches, they were often spied upon or punished for being Christian. However, officers could not spy on soldiers visiting in private homes. And our home in Sui Pak Yuen was very private, and open to all the Gurkhas. The Lord truly chose our base in Hong Kong.

The veranda was a perfect place to serve curry and rice after Sunday fellowship with Gurkhas and their families.

While we were there, one Gurkha friend described his experience.

"A Gurkha believer was in charge of pressing officers' trousers. Two fellow believers came to his room. The three prayed together.

"Suddenly the door opened. An officer found them talking to the Lord and hustled off to report them to the commander-in-charge. Back he came.

"'Give me the names of all four men who were praying,' he ordered.

"'I'm sorry, Sir, we were only three!' replied the Christian.

"'But I distinctly saw four!' huffed the officer.

"'The fourth was the Living God who is with us here in the Camp!' declared the men."

Every Sunday we met to sing and study the Word. The men came as often as their duty permitted. The large verandah around our part of the building made an ideal spot for meals and for sitting under the shade of huge nearby trees. I had endless opportunities to meet with the womenfolk in their camp homes. Many had come straight out of the hills of Nepal and needed an understanding friend and the Gospel.

In Hong Kong, we befriended many Gurkha soldiers. Some were believers, such as this one holding his Nepali Bible, the one Roy helped translate.

As we befriended many Gurkhas and their families, the light of the Gospel burned more brightly in their hearts. But they could not burn the things in- side the Gurkha camps that I was asked to burn.

Bondages Burned

The hum of glove-stitching machines in our Hong Kong Chinese neighbor's home suddenly slowed down. Even the clatter of the leather-cutting machine nearly stopped. The neighbors must have been wondering what we were burning on the trash pile, because we were singing as we fed the fire.

One of our Nepali teacher friends, Jayta, had been addicted to alcohol and chewing tobacco, and had been under severe oppression.

But all these problems are defeated foes from Jesus' viewpoint. Jesus completely overcame Satan and all his power of darkness when He died on the cross and then rose from the dead.

Jesus gave us authority over serpents, scorpions and over all the power of the enemy. So we took our stand in Jesus' name over the bondages in Jayta's life.

Jayta gave us a collection of ghost stories he had written and acted out for the military radio station. He knew he must get rid of them. So that was the reason for our first bonfire.

A few days later he handed me an enormous pile of books on the occult, palmistry, and fortune telling. Because burning trash was discouraged in the Gurkha camps, I put them in our car to burn on our trash pile.

"Lord, I claim your protection through the blood of Jesus shed for me," I prayed, as I walked away from Jayta's house.

Driving back home in our little red car, I burst into song: "In the name of Jesus, we have the victory!" Suddenly a car came speeding from behind and whizzed around me in a no-passing zone just barely avoiding a collision with an oncoming car. I thanked God for His angels protecting me.

I knew Satan was not happy over that trip. But that night we had another joyful time over a bonfire behind our home.

Then Jayta's beautiful daughter became ill. The Lord revealed there were more things to be gotten rid of in their home. As we continued to pray for cleansing of his entire house, Jayta brought out a decorative "Chinese goddess by the sea." That went out in the name of Jesus, and so did his daughter's affliction. She would one day become a teacher at the Darjeeling Hills Bible School.

However, that was not the end of bonfires or blessings.

For thirty-one long years Jayta had tried to overcome chewing tobacco. First he sucked cloves to kick the habit. Then he smoked cigarettes, and then he again resorted to cloves. But the day he received the baptism of the Holy Spirit, all desire for tobacco left him completely. "I didn't even ask for victory!" he exclaimed. He was a joyful, liberated man.

A few weeks later Roy and I were sharing Jesus with a sick friend, Maili, in the hospital The Lord led us to discuss the importance of letting go of our judgment of others and letting the Lord be the only judge. During the next few days Maili wrote down a long list of folk who had hurt or offended her during the past thirty to forty years. She forgave them one by one, letting the Lord alone be the Judge. She stuffed the list into a big envelope.

To assure her that her business with the Lord was a private confidential thing, we brought along matches and burned the sealed envelope right outside her hospital room on the rough cement verandah where she could see it all being done. It took ten matches to completely burn the thick envelope. Beautiful release and healing came soon afterward.

Then we were off to the trash pile again. It wasn't to dispose of potato peelings or an empty soup tin, but to burn Raja's book and paraphernalia of Free Masonry. What was called "Free" Masonry had bound the owner to a terrible fear of death should he break his Masonic oath. He had been in a mental hospital undergoing shock treatments. He was an alcoholic and in dreadful spiritual darkness.

As he came to Jesus in repentance and simple faith, he also received release from depression and alcohol. He realized that Jesus brings all things into the light and openness. What is not in Him is hidden in dark secrecy. The hidden Masonic vows are in direct diso-bedience to Jesus' command regarding oaths and walking in the light.

The climax of the whole affair came when Raja learned that the "sacred" and mysterious name of the god the Masons call upon, *Jaybulon*, really stood for Yah (the Hebrew God Yahweh), Bul (the Baal of the Canaanites), and On (the Egyptian god of the underworld).

In Jesus' name we bound the spirit of *Jaybulon* and reminded it that it was a defeated foe, and it had to leave because of the power of the blood of Jesus shed on the cross.

That evening Raja renounced the darkness, repented and asked us to burn the pile of books, his Masonic apron, and other paraphernalia. The power and fear of Masonry was broken. Jesus had won a great victory.

I was learning I needed a good supply of matches. I sang as I went shopping for them.

The group of Gurkhas met faithfully for four years. When one of the wives was ready for baptism, the older sergeant in the group insisted she confess all her sins to the group. We strongly opposed this. "No, no! Just let her confess them to the Lord!" Roy declared and showed scripture after scripture. But the sergeant was adamant.

Being of senior rank, he had the authority to forbid his fellow soldiers from coming to our home for fellowship, and he used it immediately. He announced, "This is our last meeting here!" Trained to respect higher rank, the Gurkhas left quietly. We were stunned, and spent many an hour in prayer for the group. Some of the faithful men would occasionally turn up for fellowship in the evening, but that was all after this sergeant closed the meetings.

Two years later, we were invited to a big Nepali party. The sergeant who had opposed us so strongly stood up to speak. He asked our forgiveness. Then he presented Roy with a kukri in a beautifully engraved case. The Lord had answered prayer, and had restored the breach.

By 1978, Paul had completed Bible school, college and seminary. Becky Ruohoniemi had finished college, nurses training and a midwifery course. They were married August 20, 1977.

Joyce Ruohoniemi and I had indeed heard from the Lord on that cold day in Darjeeling. It had been easier to teach Paul the three R's than the more difficult three L's.

The Three L's:
Listen, Learn and Love

May 24, 1978 was the day that Paul was to be ordained, but we could not attend the service. So we wrote a letter.

Dear Paul:

Sunday you are to be ordained! How we would love to be with you, but here we are a quarter of a world away. What can a missionary Mom write to her son after he has finished Bible school, college, seminary and now about to launch out to minister in far-off Nepal? You have grown up with dear Nepalis and love them. What word can I share with you?

It's so easy to think of things I wish I had taught you better when you were a little boy, like keeping your collections of rocks and stamps more orderly. But orderliness is not the first criterion for the making of a man of God, though it would surely make Becky happy.

There is something that I want to share. You have learned the three R's well. Now let me share the three L's.

I learned them from one of the most unforgettable men I have ever met, a pioneer in Muslim work, Dr. F.F. Goodsell. About a dozen of us from the four corners of the world sat in a circle as Dr. Goodsell shared his life experiences. He had hobnobbed with Schweitzer and Samuel Zwemer and knew Gandhi. He had tutored Queen Victoria's granddaughter, the Queen of Rumania, in English and had worked many years in Turkey.

I can see him even now, his snow-white hair immaculately groomed as he sat erect in a red velvet, high-backed chair. He was working a large motto, "There are no strangers, only friends we haven't met," in needlepoint as he mused over his eventful ninety-three years. He would momentarily stop the needlework and adjust his agate tiepin, as he encouraged us to have an indoor hobby and an outdoor hobby. His outdoor hobby was mountain climbing. He had climbed the Matterhorn. He told us how he wrote a page every day in his diary on the meditation he had done in the

Word that morning. He and his wife had read the Word and sung a hymn together every day of their married lives. He could not stress too strongly the power of a positive purpose in life. "Keep your goal and purpose simply Jesus!"

Then we asked him, "If you could give a brief word of advice to folk going overseas, what do you consider the most important thing to tell them?"

He held the needle poised in his curved index finger as his eyes narrowed, and he sat silent for a moment. Then he said, "I would tell them to listen, learn, and love." That's the word I would like to pass on to you and Becky.

Listen in love to the Lord, joyfully, expectantly. His sheep hear His voice.

Learn to know and to love His voice in the many ways in which He speaks. Learn to refuse your own voice and the voice of the enemy, to close the door of your spirit to all but His voice. When you hear His voice, everything is enhanced. Obey as soon as you hear His voice. Learn to listen to the silence too! The disciples began the first building committee on the mountaintop. "Let us build..." they said, and the Father promptly said, "This is My Beloved Son, listen to

Hagens' son Paul and wife Becky converse with a Gurkha soldier in Hong Kong.

Him."

Listen in love to those with whom you live. Listen to the way they say things, but listen also to what their heart is saying.

"Learn of Me," Jesus says, "for I am meek and lowly." He could of His own self do nothing, neither pray nor teach nor heal, and He wasn't afraid to say so. He depended one hundred percent on the Father. Then He said, "Learn of Me." He learned obedience by not doing the things He could have done. There will be many times you would rather do things the Western way. But for His sake and the sake of those with whom you live and move, learn of Him and of them. Strive to learn to understand them.

Love! Love the Father, love the Son, love the Spirit of God with all your heart. Keep head-over-heels in love with Him. Love, Paul, with a Calvary love that outshines all biblical knowledge, cultural knowledge, self-knowledge. See each person as one dearly loved of the Father, as one for whom Jesus died. Pray daily that love might be in all your thoughts, that love might shine through your eyes, that love might learn the heart-cry of the other, that love might be in your touch and talk and walk. Pray that you might be an embodiment of the Father's love wherever you go. For our Father God is Love. Your love may be rejected by some to whom you go. Count that as all joy and go on loving as Jesus did.

This is my continual prayer for you, Paul, that you may listen to, learn from and love Him above all else; and as you do that, you will listen to, learn from, and love those to whom you go.

In His overwhelming love,

Mom

The fruit of the three L's would be seen years later in an unusual torch procession.

Seeing Through Open Doors

In 1998 twenty young men, all carrying torches, gathered in a Siliguri church. This was not a replay of the Olympics dedicated to the Greek god Zeus. Instead it was a far more important event: the Gospel torch of Jesus Christ was being lit throughout the Himalayas. One by one the twenty men committed their way to the Lord. The church prayed over them. Their kerosene torches were lit and they were off.

The young men had about fifty miles to cover in four days as they began their procession up the mountains to Darjeeling. All along the way the churches en route participated in public rallies, in prayer

At the Himalyan Congress on Evangelism, 1998, Darjeeling, India, 1200 Nepali leaders gathered to declare that Nepalis are now a sending rather than receiving people. Dr Thomas Wang led the Nepalis in blessing those who pioneered the work in Nepal. Roy and Alma Hagen, on the left, are wearing the Tibetan kadas, an honorific scarf comparable to the Hawaiian lei.

meetings, and in replenishing the oil for their torches.

The torches were symbolic of the fire of the Holy Spirit being lit in the Himalayas and a new missionary spirit being lit in the hearts of Nepali and Himalayan Christians. The twenty made their way triumphantly into the big hall, as the opening song of the Himalayan Congress on Evangelism (HIM-COE 98) began. Some 1,200 participants, leaders of Nepali churches, gathered from across Nepal, Sikkim, the Darjeeling hills, Bhutan, and northwest and northeast India. There were also Nepali representatives from Burma, Singapore, Taiwan and Scotland.

Roy and I had been invited, along with eleven other pioneer missionary guests, to participate in this awesome conference. It was almost "too good to be true" to see these hundreds of Nepali believers, all keen to share the good news of Jesus. Even when becoming a Christian and being baptized meant a possible year or more in prison, many had still surrendered their lives to Jesus as Lord. For some it meant losing their inheritance or being thrown out by the family. Some were thrown out of their villages and could not drink water from the village well because they were believers. But they had received forgiveness of sins, the gift of eternal life, peace, truth, and new life. They no longer feared the Hindu spirits and "gods". They were not to be deterred.

Over the last fifty years the church in Nepal had grown phenomenally, especially since the change in Nepal's Constitution. From east to west it has grown, and not because of one particular leader or one particular denomination, rather, it has grown by the initiative and power of God's Holy Spirit working among the Nepalis.

The theme rang out: "Himalayan Peoples – Missionary Peoples!" No longer were the Nepalis to be a mission-receiving people but a ministering, sending people.

Roy and I sat weeping, weeping with joy at all God had done since we first landed in Calcutta forty-seven years earlier. One after another of the believers came up to us to say, "I studied in Darjeeling Hills Bible School," or to say, "I'm so-and-so's son." They had been just youngsters the last time we saw them, and now they were busy in the kingdom of God. The torch had been passed on!

The Bible school graduates, some five hundred, had become the backbone of the Nepali church worldwide, one of the fastest growing churches in the world. There were an estimated 500,000 believers in

Nepal in 1998.

Wherever Christians were multiplying and growing in maturity and skills, there were more and better services to care for people. Numerous Christian schools have sprung up. Many new orphanages give hope to children in a country where orphans used to be left to fend for themselves. There are homes to help rehabilitate girls rescued from brothels in India. Many churches have established living places for the elderly who have no family to care for them. The value placed on girls and women has changed dramatically. The caste system is breaking down as Christian Brahmins receive communion from "untouchable" brothers in Christ. By 2005, the literacy rate in Nepal had grown from 2% to 62% for men, and to 28% for women.

God had opened the door, He had been faithful, and we had walked through!

> *"Not to us, O Lord,*
> *not to us but to Your name be the glory,*
> *because of Your love and faithfulness."*
>
> *Psalm115:1*

> *"I looked, and lo, a door standing open in heaven . . . "*
> *Revelation 4:1*

> *"I saw a Lamb standing as though it were slain.*
> *You purchased men unto God from every tribe*
> *and language and people and nation!"*
> *Revelation 5:16*

There will come a day when we will see them streaming through that open door.

Hallelujah!

Epilogue

What further shall I say? Change and growth has been continual.

We knew we were to teach English in China. In order to do so, we resigned our legal affiliation with missions organizations so that we could honestly say, "We are English teachers."

Our season in China was marked by great contrast. Our Mandarin teacher in Hong Kong came from an influential family in China. Her mother was head of a cultural department, and would often give us tickets for front-row theater seats for the most special events.

Our official invitation to teach had come from the Chinese Coal Mining Ministry. After our visas were stamped in our passports, everything changed. The Coal Mining Ministry stalled in appointing us to a specific position. In faith, we proceeded to Beijing. We spent nine months teaching diplomats from many countries while we waited. An old Chinese grandfather with whom Roy visited weekly told him of the Chinese proverb: "Only the one who ties the bell on the cat can take the bell off the cat." We knew we had to go back to the ones who had originally invited us.

Roy wrote a letter explaining our position and it was passed to upper leadership in the nation. Soon, the Coal Mining Ministry had a job for us in the north of China. During the initial interview with the officials from the English Department, the first thing they said was, "We have students from all over China." We were not surprised because we had earlier received a prophecy that our students would come from all over China.

Months later we learned the reason we had so much difficulty. Addressing a letter to us care of the Coal Mining Ministry, a Gurkha had written to us using the Nepali script. On the back of the envelope he had drawn a large cross adding in English, "Jesus is Lord." That was not appreciated by the strong Communist administration in 1981.

After our memorable stint of teaching English in China, the Lord led us to "the land of the lotus." In expensive Japan we were privileged to earn our bread and butter by teaching English to Kindergartners, as well as to students of all ages. Our training in teaching English as a second language came in good stead. And Mary Verghese's prophetic word ten years before that we would teach Asian children was fulfilled.

Then Nepal's Door Opened

Margaret Luttio (nee Birkedal), with whom I worked in Chicago years earlier, served in Japan with her husband Phil for many years. She began Women's Aglow there, and became National Aglow Coordinator. When they retired, I was asked to continue her ministry as Aglow Coordinator. This entailed traveling the length and breadth of Japan, meeting with dear Japanese women hungry for the Lord and helping to set up new chapters of Women's Aglow.

Roy taught English as well and helped several pastors who were busy with translation work to better understand the English idioms. We were asked to house-sit a beautifully furnished Japanese home for six years. God supplied in ways exceedingly abundantly above all we could ask or imagine, and He received the glory!

While in Japan, one morning the Lord spoke clearly to me through Exodus 23:25 (Amplified Version): "Worship the Lord your God. . . I will take sickness from your midst. . . I will give you a full life span." A few minutes later the phone rang. The doctor to whom I had gone for an exam said, "You have carcinoma of the colon." I continued to worship the Lord and went to Greece for an alternative cancer treatment. I have been cancer free ever since, all praise to God alone.

In 1994 we returned to retire in the States. This was not entirely uneventful. One bitterly cold morning in Minneapolis I was scheduled for a cholesterol blood test. At 20°F below zero (-28.9°C) our car would not start, so I bundled up and walked five blocks to the clinic.

While returning home, I heard a strange sound behind me. Turning around, I was confronted by a man pointing a gun at me, demanding, "Give me your purse!"

In an instant I commanded, "In Jesus' name you GO!" He fled across the street and behind a nearby house. The name of Jesus is as powerful in the States as in Asia!

The burden and concern for the Nepalis, Chinese and Japanese has not abated. We continue to pray especially for Nepal, going through the traumatic life-threatening upheaval of violent Maoist insurgents.

In 2004 we were invited to attend the fiftieth anniversary of the Darjeeling Hills Bible School that Roy founded. Even though we could not attend, we praise God for His faithfulness to the school all through these years. The school is upgrading its curriculum to the Bachelor of Theology (B.Th.) level. When we think back on all the blessings of the DHBS, we cannot help but thank our many WMPL friends who stood by us in prayer and support over these many years. We know they will continue their ministry before the Lord.

Now Roy and I make our home in Atlanta, Georgia.

Our son David is currently a research engineer developing cleaner and more cost effective power systems. He resides in Goshen, Indiana, with his water-color-artist wife Cathy and harp-playing daughter Anna.

Paul and Becky spent over thirteen years in western Nepal, working with tuberculosis and leprosy control and with Bible translation. Presently Paul is pastor of St. Peter's Lutheran Church, a congregation of primarily Caribbean immigrants, in the Bronx, New York, another real mission field. His three oldest, Tim, Karis, and Kaisa are college graduates; Nahan is starting college.

Our son Ken is a Medical Technician in Eggleston Children's Hospital in Atlanta, Georgia, where he and his counselor wife, Linda, reside.

Son Karl is also in Atlanta, a Professor of Bio-Inorganic Chemistry at Emory University. His wife, Kimberly, teaches in Emory's Department of Behavioral Science and Health Education and co-ordinates AIDS research.

All our lives have been wonderfully enriched by our life overseas. When our families all get together, there is plenty of singing, the menu is curry and rice, and the conversation is sprinkled with Nepali. Our one desire is that we as a family may give God the glory, of which He is so worthy.

Glossary

Adult Literacy Teacher Training. Training teachers to teach literacy with pictures.

Ajmir. A state in NW India.

Augustana Academy. Lutheran High School, formerly in Canton, South Dakota.

Axelson, Alice. American missionary nurse working among the Santals in India.

Bahadur. Nepali for "brave." Hagens' cook and errand man.

Bajay. Darjeeling Nepali for grandfather or priest.

Berg, Alvin "Al" and Vallie. American WMPL missionaries.

Bhattarai, K.P. Highly gifted Nepali poet, writer, and translator.

Birendra (Rongong). Originally from Kalimpong, gifted blind singer and sitar player.

Birkedal, Margaret. Alma's co-worker in 1944. Married Phil Luttio, missionary to Japan.

Bisset, Peter. British member of International Nepal Fellowship staff.

Blackout. An elimination or concealing of all lights possibly visible to an enemy.

Buckwalter, Allen and Leoda. Founder/director of Far East Broadcasting Associates, India.

Boju. Darjeeling Nepali for grandmother or priestess.

Brokke, Harold. Student of St. Olaf College, later teacher and administrator at Bethany Fellowship, Minneapolis.

Buchen, Frieda Martini. Alma Hagen's mother.

Buchen. A town in Westfalen, Germany, named after Dr. Buchen's ancestors. German for Beech tree.

Budhiman. A Nepali gentleman who was the first printer for the Mirik Press and J.J.P.

Bunny. Nickname for Bernice Gullickson, English teacher at Augustana Academy and later, a missionary to Afghanistan.

Byatt, Ron. British missionary who assembled the Nepali hymn book. Pioneer teacher in Amp Pipal.

Car jack. An implement used to lift a car in order to change tires.

Carlson, Lillian. WMPL missionary teacher in Kalimpong, working among Tibetans.

Chatra Niwas. residence on a Mirik hillside, later part of Darjeeling Hills Bible School.

Christiansen, Dorothy. WMPL missionary nurse working among Tibetans in Kalimpong.

Church, Dr. Joe. Medical missionary doctor from Rwanda.

Glossary

Civil Surgeon. Chief medical surgeon of a city.

Cook, Hope. American heiress of Cook Travels who became the Gyalmo, Queen of Sikkim.

Dan Mit Rongong. A Lepcha lady who served as caretaker for Hagen children and later became Hagens' cook.

Das, Robi. Director of Calcutta's Bible Society.

DHBS. Darjeeling Hills Bible School, the first Bible School that taught Nepalis in their own language, started by Roy Hagen in Mirik, India, in 1954.

Duncan, "Daddy." Senior Scots Presbyterian missionary.

Ebenezer Home. A retirement home for senior citizens.

Electrocardiogram. A graph showing a person's heart activity.

FEBA. Far East Broadcasting Associates (of India). The Indian branch of Far East Broadcasting Co.

Festival of Lights. "Diwali." Hindu holiday to worship Lakshmi, the Hindu goddess of wealth.

Fleming, Dr. Bob. An American ornithologist who began Protestant medical work in Kathmandu with his wife, Dr. Bethel Fleming, a medical doctor.

Fowler, Meridel. Canadian nurse working for Mother Theresa in Darjeeling. Later became Mrs. Jay Rawlings.

Franklin, Benjamin. American statesman, scientist, inventor and writer, 1706-1790.

Garrison, Mr. A. J. Retired missionary from South India who settled in Gorakhpur with prayer focus on Nepal.

Ghorahi. A town in west Nepal where Betty Bailey and team were stationed.

Green Pastures. Leprosarium in Pokhara, Nepal

Grimsrud, Becky. First WMPL missionary nurse to work among Nepalis in Darjeeling, Dist.

Gurkha. A Nepali soldier.

Gurung Cottage. Name of two-storey house where WMPL missionary ladies lived and where DHBS classes began.

Gyalmo. Sikkimese name for Queen.

Hagen, Christian. Roy Hagen's father.

Hagen, David. Oldest son of the Roy Hagens.

Hagen, Ingeborg. Roy Hagen's mother.

Hagen, Karl. Youngest son of the Roy Hagens.

Hagen, Kenneth. Third son of the Roy Hagens.

Hagen, Paul. Second son of the Roy Hagens. Married Becky Ruohoneimi, and worked in western Nepal for 17 years.

Hansen, Betty. WMPL missionary who married Canadian missionary

Herman Simrose.

Hartal. A total strike when no vehicles are allowed to move, no shops allowed to open.

Hasselquist, Millie. WMPL missionary in Darjeeling District, now Mrs. Luverne Tengbom.

Haukvik, Art and Nora. Farmers near Hanska, Minnesota.

Heflin, Ruth. Pentecostal traveling missionary.

Heidelberg Press. Automatic printing press installed at Jiwan Jyoti Prakashan in Darjeeling.

Hillary, Edmund. A New Zealand beekeeper, who along with Tenzing Norgay, were the first two to reach the summit of Mt. Everest in 1953.

HIM-COE/98. Himalayan Congress on Evangelism, 1998.

Himalaya Mountains. Highest mountains in the world that form natural border between India, Nepal, and China.

Hindi. The common language of North India.

Hjelmervik, Clarence and Helen. WMPL missionaries moved from west China to Darjeeling because of Communist takeover in China.

Himalaya Prakashan (HP). "Himalayan Publishers" organized by Roy Hagen in Kathmandu to do graphic printing inside Nepal.

Jayta. Oldest son in Nepali.

Jayti. Oldest daughter in Nepali.

Jiwan Jyoti Prakashan. "Light of Life Publishers", started by Roy Hagen to provide Christian literature for Nepalis.

Kamal. Nepali man's name.

Kanchenjunga. Third highest mountain in the world, easily viewed from Darjeeling.

Kanchi Maya. Nepali woman's name. Kanchi means youngest daughter, Maya means love.

Karthak, Pastor Robert. Much respected senior pastor of Gyaneshwar church in Kathmandu.

Karthak, Solon. Valued Nepali writer.

Kathmandu. Capitol of Nepal.

Kennedy School of Missions. Graduate level institute for world languages and cultures.

Knights of Luther. A team of Christian boys focused on singing and witnessing for Christ.

Kukri. A commonly used foot-long Nepali knife.

Kutchery. Nepali name for court house.

Lama. A Buddhist priest or monk.

Land Rover. A sturdy vehicle built by Land Rover of UK. Larger than a jeep, often used in difficult terrain.

Landsverks, Ob and Helen. American missionaries under the Santal Mission.

Glossary

Laubach, Dr. Frank. World renowned "Apostle of Literacy," teaching illiterates their own language from pictures.

LEAP. Literacy and Education Advance Program, the literacy branch of the NISS.

Lindell, Jonathan. Brother of the founder of Lutheran World Crusade, Paul Lindell. First WMPL missionary to go to Darjeeling District. Later became administrator and teacher in the UMN. Started UMN work in Amp Pipal.

Luther's Catechism. A small booklet of basic Christian beliefs.

Lutheran World Crusade. A mission organization focused on the heart of central Asia, central Africa and South America. Later joined the World Mission Prayer League.

Machan. A wooden frame bed with woven strings as mattress.

Madar TB Sanatorium. A Methodist hospital for treating tuberculosis patients.

Madar, Ajmir. Location of TB Sanatorium.

Magar. A Nepali tribal group.

Maharajah. Indian name for a prince or king who rules an Indian state.

Mahendra Kumar. Nepali Principal of Darjeeling Boys School.

Mahout. Elephant driver or keeper.

Maila. Nepali name for second son.

Maili. Nepali name for second daughter. Hagen household helper.

Manab, Pooba. Kathmandu teacher, political activist called "Sadhuji" by Darjeeling friends.

Manaen, Theodore. Former Secretary of the All India Congress Party, Member of Parliament, and Associate Director of WMPL, retired.

Managing Board. A group of Christian leaders directing the affairs of the Bible School.

Mansubba Rai. Member of first class of DHBS.

Manu. Short for Mansubba (Rai). At baptism, she chose Martha as her new name.

Maraj, Jonathan. A WMPL missionary originally from Trinidad.

Meinel, Drs. Aden and Marjorie. University of Arizona and JPL Astronomers, space, and solar energy scientists. Advisors for United States National Aeronautics and Space Administration (NASA).

Michael, Dr. Indian Tuberculosis TB specialist.

Mirik. Village 27 miles from Darjeeling on Nepal Border.

Missahib. Indian name given to unmarried foreign woman.

Momsey. Alma's affectionate name for her mother, Frieda Martini Buchen.

Monastery. A building or residence for those devoted to religion.

Moran, Father M. Founder of St. Xavier's School in Kathmandu.

Mud Stove. A cooking stove made of stones covered with mud clay.

Mukhia, Shilling. TB patient. Later became DHBS student and pioneer in Amp Pipal, Nepal.

Mukhia, Auntie Ruth. Pastor D.H. Mukhia's sister, a retired nurse.

Mukhia, D.H. Pastor of Darjeeling St. Colomba's Church.

Mukhia, David. Nepali pastor of first Christian group to go into Nepal.

Nagenda, William. African missionary from Rwanda.

Namgyal, Gyalmo. Queen of Sikkim, formerly Hope Cook.

NEFA. North East Frontier Area, now called Arunchal Pradesh, east of Bhutan.

Nepal Border Fellowship. A fellowship of Mission organizations focused on reaching Nepalis.

Nepali Isai Sahitya Sangha (NISS). Nepali Christian Literature Society.

Nepali Girls Boarding School. A school in Darjeeling operated by the Scots Presbyterian Mission.

Nirvana. The condition of escape from the cycle of reincarnation by the extinction of desire, suffering and individual consciousness, particularly in Hinduism and Buddhism, supposedly a condition of peace or bliss.

Norgay, Tenzing. Nepali Sherpa who conquered Everest for the first time with New Zealander Edmund Hillary.

Norwegian, The. Monrad Ulvesetter who worked with WMPL among Tibetans.

O'Hanlon, Dr. Lily. (Known as "Pat.") Medical doctor and leader of the Nepal Evangelistic Band, first Protestant missionaries to work in Pokhara, Nepal. The NEB later became the International Nepal Fellowship.

Oliver, Ernest. Brethren missionary with British background.

Orthopedic surgeon. A doctor who specializes in treating injuries of the bones, joints and muscles.

Overvold, Ruth. WMPL missionary nurse.

Palau. Indian fried rice dish.

Patterson, Meg. Scottish medical doctor, wife of famed writer George Patterson.

Patterson, Miss. New Zealand missionary to Sikkim.

Pavilion. A large tent.

Peroneal tendon. An important tendon near the fibula in the ankle area.

POL-MIL. Police Military base in Fanling, HK, near Hagens' home.

Pradhan, Unamani. One of original group of literacy trainees in DHBS. Worked in Amp Pipal. Later married Sunhang Sodemba. teacher in Amp Pipal, Nepal.

Pradhan, Ganga Prasad. A Newar born in Kathmandu who became the second Nepali Christian in the Darjeeling Nepali church.

Premi. Nepali word for loving. Pastor David Mukhia's wife.

Punkabari Road. Alternate road between Kurseong and Siliguri on the plains.

Puran. Hindu Scriptures.

Putz, Herta. Alma's German cousin.

Raddon, Jean. A member of the first Protestant team to go into Pokhara with Dr. Lily O'Hanlon.

Rai, Bir Bahadur. A DHBS student later to be imprisoned in Tansen for his faith.

Rai, Alice. A trained teacher. One of the first graduates of Mirik Bible School.

Rai, L.B. NISS office manager.

Ram, Ralla. Director of Regions Beyond Mission

Rana, Col. Nararaj Shamshere Jung Bahadur. One of the Bible Translators, from Kathmandu.

Robinson, Bishop. Anglican leader of North India.

Rongong, Arnold. NISS editor.

Rongong, Adon. Gifted Nepali writer who opened Patan Book House, which became the Ekta Books publishing house.

Ruohoniemi, San. A UMN Hospital Administrator in Kathmandu. Wife: Joyce.

Rusks. A sweet raised bread toasted in an oven until brown and crisp.

Sadiron. A heavy solid flat iron, pointed at both ends, heated over a fire or on a stove.

Sandakphu. Highest point in Darjeeling District.

Sangati. First Nepali Christian Magazine.

Shaw, Gwen. Founder of End-Time Handmaidens.

Sikkim. A small state north of Darjeeling District, India, formerly ruled by a Buddhist king (or Maharajah).

Silage. Course green food for cattle.

Siliguri. A large city, important railhead on the plains, about 50 miles from Darjeeling.

Silo. An air tight tower in which green fodder is preserved for cattle.

Simrose, Herman. A Canadian WMPL missionary working with agricultural demonstration projects.

Sri Tashi Namgyal. Ruler of Sikkim.

St. Joseph's Mount. Name of house where WMPL missionaries in Darjeeling first resided.

Steele, Hilda. Co-worker of Dr. Lily O'Hanlon in Pokhara, Nepal, member of the first Protestant team to go into Nepal.

Stoa, Pastor. Lutheran pastor of Norwegian ancestry.

Sui Pak Yuen. A beautiful Chinese home and garden in Fanling, HK.

SIL International (Summer Institute of Linguistics) Organization facilitating language-based development, serving the peoples of the world through research, translation, and literacy. www.SIL.org

Swenson, Fran. WMPL missionary who first taught at Mirik Bible School before working with the United Mission to Nepal.

Tashi. Fictitious name for Tibetan trader who sold a jeep to WMPL.

Thapa, Tej (Maila). Kamala's mother's son, later called Jonathan Thapa.

Thurbo Tea Estate. A tea plantation located on the edge of Mirik.

Tonga. A two-wheeled Indian horse drawn cart with seats for passengers.

Tonsillitis. An inflamation of the tonsils.

Treasure Hunt. Name of weekly Children's radio program in English by Alma Hagen broadcast by FEBA.

Trough. A long narrow container holding food for animals.

Tshering, Subit. First seminary-trained Nepali pastor and teacher at DHBS (Mirik Bible School).

Tuberculosis. (TB) Lung infection. Greatest cause of death in the world until HIV/AIDS. Common in Nepal & India.

Turnbull Boys School. Operated in Darjeeling by the Scots Presbyterian Mission.

Ulvesetter, Monrad. A Norwegian affiliated with Nepal WMPL.

UMN. United Mission to Nepal. Formerly known as United Christian Mission.

Vincent, Alan. British-born missionary with present worldwide ministry.

Wax, sealing. Wax used for sealing letters, often stamped with a signet ring.

World Mission Prayer League (WMPL). A Lutheran faith based mission, in three continents, headquartered in Minneapolis, Minnesota, USA. Hagen's initial sending agency.

Wycliffe Bible Translators. Organization focused on translating the Bible into languages without Bible translations.

Printed in the United States
57358LVS00006B/151-1011